THE COMMERCE AND NAVIGATION OF THE ERYTHRAEAN SEA

LECTOR HOUSE PUBLIC DOMAIN WORKS

THE COMMERCE AND NAVIGATION OF THE ERYTHRAEAN SEA

ANONYMOUS, JOHN WATSON MCCRINDLE

ISBN: 978-93-5614-458-3

Published: 1879

LECTOR HOUSE LLP
E-MAIL: lectorpublishing@gmail.com

THE COMMERCE AND NAVIGATION OF THE ERYTHRÆAN SEA;

BEING A TRANSLATION OF THE PERIPLUS MARIS ERYTHRÆI, BY AN ANONYMOUS WRITER, AND OF ARRIAN'S ACCOUNT OF THE VOYAGE OF NEARKHOS, FROM THE MOUTH OF THE INDUS TO THE HEAD OF THE PERSIAN GULF.

WITH INTRODUCTIONS, COMMENTARY, NOTES, AND INDEX.
BY
J. W. MCCRINDLE, M.A. EDIN.,

PRINCIPAL OF THE GOVERNMENT COLLEGE, PATNA; MEMBER OF THE COUNCIL OF THE UNIVERSITY OF EDINBURGH; FELLOW OF THE CALCUTTA UNIVERSITY.

(Reprinted, with additions, from the Indian Antiquary.)

1879.

PREFACE.

In the Preface to my former work, "Ancient India as described by Megasthenês and Arrian," I informed the reader that it was my intention to publish from time to time translations of the Greek and Latin works which relate to ancient India, until the series should be exhausted, and the present volume is the second instalment towards the fulfilment of that undertaking. It contains a translation of the *Periplûs* (*i. e. Circumnavigation*) *of the Erythræan Sea*, together with a translation of the second part of the *Indika* of Arrian describing the celebrated voyage made by Nearkhos from the mouth of the Indus to the head of the Persian Gulf. Arrian's narrative, copied from the Journal of the voyage written by Nearkhos himself, forms an admirable supplement to the Periplûs, as it contains a minute description of a part of the Erythræan Coast which is merely glanced at by the author of that work. The translations have been prepared from the most approved texts. The notes, in a few instances only, bear upon points of textual criticism, their main object being to present in a concise form for popular reading the most recent results of learned enquiry directed to verify, correct, or otherwise illustrate the contents of the narratives.

The warm and unanimous approbation bestowed upon the first volume of this series, both by the Press in this country and at home, has given me great encouragement to proceed with the undertaking, and a third volume is now in preparation, to contain the *Indika* of Ktêsias and the account of India given by Strabo in the 15th Book of his Geography.

Patna College, June 1879.

CONTENTS

ANONYMI [ARRIANI UT FERTUR]
PERIPLUS MARIS ERYTHRÆI.

TRANSLATED FROM THE TEXT

As given in the *Geographi Græci Minores*, edited by
C. Muller: Paris, 1855.

WITH INTRODUCTION
AND COMMENTARY.

PERIPLUS OF THE ERYTHRÆAN SEA.

INTRODUCTION.[1]

The *Periplûs of the Erythræan Sea* is the title prefixed to a work which contains the best account of the commerce carried on from the Red Sea and the coast of Africa to the East Indies during the time that Egypt was a province of the Roman empire. The E r y t h r æ a n   S e a was an appellation given in those days to the whole expanse of ocean reaching from the coast of Africa to the utmost boundary of ancient knowledge on the East—an appellation in all appearance deduced from the entrance into it by the Straits of the Red Sea, styled E r y t h r a by the Greeks, and not excluding the Gulf of Persia.

The author was a Greek merchant, who in the first century of the Christian era had, it would appear, settled at B e r e n î k ê , a great seaport situated in the southern extremity of Egypt, whence he made commercial voyages which carried him to the seaports of Eastern Africa as far as A z a n i a , and to those of Arabia as far as K a n ê , whence, by taking advantage of the south-west monsoon, he crossed over to the ports lying on the western shores of India. Having made careful observations and inquiries regarding the navigation and commerce of these countries, he committed to writing, for the benefit of other merchants, the knowledge which he had thus acquired. Much cannot be said in praise of the style in which he writes. It is marked by a rude simplicity, which shows that he was not a man of literary culture, but in fact a mere man of business, who in composing restricts himself to a narrow round of set phrases, and is indifferent alike to grace, freedom, or variety of expression. It shows further that he was a Greek settled in Egypt, and that he must have belonged to an isolated community of his countrymen, whose speech had become corrupt by much intercourse with foreigners. It presents a very striking contrast to the rhetorical diction which A g a t h a r k h i d ê s , a great master of all the tricks of speech, employs in his description of the Erythræan. For all shortcomings, however, in the style of the work, there is ample compensation in the fulness, variety, accuracy, and utility of the information which it conveys. Such indeed is its superiority on these points that it must be reckoned as a most precious treasure: for to it we are indebted far more than to any other work for most of our knowledge of the remote shores of Eastern Africa, and the marts of India, and the condition of ancient commerce in these parts of the world.

---

[1] The Introduction and Commentary embody the main substance of Müller's Prolegomena and Notes to the *Periplûs*, and of Vincent's *Commerce and Navigation of the Ancients* so far as it relates specially to that work. The most recent authorities accessible have, however, been also consulted, and the result of their inquiries noted. I may mention particularly Bishop Caldwell's Dravidian Grammar, to which I am indebted for the identification of places on the Malabar and Coromandel coasts.

The name of the author is unknown. In the Heidelberg MS., which alone has preserved the little work, and contains it after the *Periplûs* of Arrian, the title given is Αρριανου περιπλους της' Ερυθρας θαλασσης. Trusting to the correctness of this title, Stuckius attributed the work to A r r i a n of Nikomedia, and Fabricius to another Arrian who belonged to Alexandria. No one, however, who knows how ancient books are usually treated can fail to see what the real fact here is, viz. that since not only the *Periplûs Maris Erythræi*, but also the *Anonymi Periplûs Ponti Euxini* (whereof the latter part occurs in the Heidelberg MS. before Arrian's *Ponti Periplûs*) are attributed to Arrian, and the different Arrians are not distinguished by any indications afforded by the titles, there can be no doubt that the well-known name of the Nikomedian writer was transferred to the books placed in juxtaposition to his proper works, by the arbitrary judgment of the librarians. In fact it very often happens that short works written by different authors are all referred to one and the same author, especially if they treat of the same subject and are published conjointly in the same volume. But in the case of the work before us, any one would have all the more readily ascribed it to Arrian who had heard by report anything of the *Paraplûs* of the Erythræan Sea described in that author's *Indika*. On this point there is the utmost unanimity of opinion among writers.

That the author, whatever may have been his name, lived in Egypt, is manifest. Thus he says in § 29: "Several of the trees *with us* in Egypt weep gum," and he joins the names of the Egyptian months with the Roman, as may be seen by referring to §§ 6, 39, 49, and 56. The place in which he was settled was probably Berenîkê, since it was from that port he embarked on his voyages to Africa and Arabia, and since he speaks of the one coast as on the right from Berenîkê, and the other on the left. The whole tenor of the work proclaims that he must have been a merchant. That the entire work is not a mere compilation from the narratives or journals of other merchants and navigators, but that the author had himself visited some of the seats of trade which he describes, is in itself probable, and is indicated in § 20, where, contrary to the custom of the ancient writers, he speaks in his own person:—"In sailing south, therefore, *we* stand off from the shore and keep *our* course down the middle of the gulf." Compare with this what is said in § 48: προς την εμποριαν την ἑμετεραν.

As regards the age to which the writer belonged: it is first of all evident that he wrote after the times of Augustus, since in § 23 mention is made of the Roman Emperors. That he was older, however, than P t o l e m y the Geographer, is proved by his geography, which knows nothing of India beyond the Ganges except the traditional account current from the days of Eratosthenês to those of Pliny, while it is evident that Ptolemy possessed much more accurate information regarding these parts. It confirms this view that while our author calls the island of Ceylon P a l a i s i m o u n d o u , Ptolemy calls it by the name subsequently given to it—S a l i k ê . Again, from § 19, it is evident that he wrote before the kingdom of the Nubathœans was abolished by the Romans. Moreover Pliny (VI. xxvi. 101), in proceeding to describe the navigation to the marts of India by the direct route across the ocean with the wind called Hippalos, writes to this effect:—"And for a long time this was the mode of navigation, until a merchant discovered a compendious route whereby India was brought so near that to trade thither became very lucrative. For, every year a fleet is despatched, carrying on board companies of archers, since the Indian seas are much infested by pirates. Nor will a description of the whole voyage from Egypt tire the reader, since now for the first time correct information regarding it has been made public." Compare with this the statement of the *Periplûs* in § 57, and it will be apparent that while this route to India had only just come into use in the time of Pliny, it had been for some time in use in the days of our author. Now, as P l i n y died in 79 A.D., and had completed his work two years previously, it may be inferred that he had written the 6th book of his *Natural History* before our author wrote his work. A still more definite indication of his date is furnished in § 5, where Z o s k a l ê s is mentioned as reigning in his times over the Auxumitae. Now in a list of the early kings of Abyssinia the name of Z a - H a k a l e occurs, who must have reigned from 77 to 89 A.D. This Z a - H a k a l e is doubtless the Z o s k a l ê s of the *Periplûs*, and was the contemporary of the emperors Vespasian, Titus, and Domitian. We conclude, therefore, that the *Periplûs* was written a little after the death of Pliny, between the years A.D. 80-89.

Opinions on this point, however, have varied considerably. Salmasius thought that Pliny and our author wrote at the same time, though their accounts of the same things are often contradictory. In support of this view he adduces the statement of the *Periplûs* (§ 54), "M u z i r i s , a place in India, is in the kingdom of Kêprobotres," when compared with the statement of Pliny (VI. xxvi. 104), "C œ l o b o t h r a s was reigning there when I committed this to writing;" and argues that since K ê p r o - b o t r e s and C œ l o b o t h r a s are but different forms of the same name, the two authors must have been contemporary. The inference is, however, unwarrantable, since the name in question, like that of P a n d i ô n , was a common appellation of the kings who ruled over that part of India.

Dodwell, again, was of opinion that the *Periplûs* was written after the year A.D. 161, when Marcus Aurelius and Lucius Verus were joint emperors. He bases, in the first place, his defence of this view on the statement in § 26: "Not long before our own times the Emperor (Καῖσαρ) destroyed the place," viz. E u d a i m ó n - A r a - b i a , now Aden. This emperor he supposes must have been Trajan, who, according to Eutropius (VIII. 3), reduced Arabia to the form of a province. Eutropius, however, meant by Arabia only that small part of it which adjoins Syria. This Dod-well not only denies, but also asserts that the conquest of Trajan embraced the whole of the Peninsula — a sweeping inference, which he bases on a single passage in the *Periplûs* (§ 16) where the south part of Arabia is called ἡ πρώτη Ἀραβία, "the First Arabia." From this expression he gathers that Trajan, after his conquest of the country, had divided it into several provinces, designated according to the order in which they were constituted. The language of the *Periplûs*, however, forbids us to suppose that there is here any reference to a Roman province. What the passage states is that A z a n i a (in Africa) was by ancient right subject to the kingdom τῆς πρώτης γινομένης (λεγομένης according to Dodwell) Ἀραβίας, and was ruled by the despot of M a p h a r i t i s .

Dodwell next defends the date he has fixed on by the passage in § 23, where it is said that K h a r i b a ë l sought by frequent gifts and embassies to gain the friendship of the emperors (τῶν αὐτοκρατόρων). He thinks that the time is here indicated when M. Aurelius and L. Verus were reigning conjointly, A.D. 161-181. There is no need, however, to put this construction on the words, which may without any impropriety be taken to mean '*the emperors for the time being*,' viz. Vespasian, Titus, and Domitian.

Vincent adopted the opinion of Salmasius regarding the date of the work, but thinks that the Kaîsar mentioned in § 26 was Claudius. "The Romans," he says, "from the time they first entered Arabia under Ælius Gallus, had always maintained a footing on the coast of the Red Sea. They had a garrison at L e u k ê   K ô m ê , in Nabathaea, where they collected the customs; and it is apparent that they extended their power down the gulf and to the ports of the ocean in the reign of Claudius, as the freedman of A n n i u s   P l o c a m u s   was in the act of collecting the tributes there when he was carried out to sea and over to T a p r o b a n ê . If we add to this the discovery of Hippalus in the same reign, we find a better reason for the destruction of Aden at this time than at any other." The assertion in this extract that the garrison and custom-house at L e u k ê   K ô m ê   belonged to the Romans is not warranted by the language of the *Periplûs*, which in fact shows that they belonged to M a l i k h o s   the king of the Nabathæans. Again, it is a mere conjecture that the voyage which the freedman of Plocamus (who, according to Pliny, farmed the revenues of the Red Sea) was making along the coast of Arabia, when he was carried away by the monsoon to Taprobanê, was a voyage undertaken to collect the revenues due to the Roman treasury. With regard to the word Καῖσαρ, which has occasioned so much perplexity, it is most probably a corrupt reading in a text notorious for its corruptness. The proper reading may perhaps be ΕΛΙΣΑΡ. At any rate, had one of the emperors in reality destroyed Aden, it is unlikely that their historians would have failed to mention such an important fact.

Schwanbeck, although he saw the weakness of the arguments with which Salmasius and Vincent endeavoured to establish their position, nevertheless thought that our author lived in the age of Pliny and wrote a little before him, because those particulars regarding the Indian navigation which Pliny says became known in his age agree, on the whole, so well with the statement in the *Periplûs* that they must have been extracted therefrom. No doubt there are, he allows, some discrepancies; but those, he thinks, may be ascribed to the haste or negligence of the copyist. A careful examination, however, of parallel passages in Pliny and the *Periplûs* show this assertion to be untenable. Vincent himself speaks with caution on this point:—"There is," he says, "no absolute proof that either copied from the other. But those who are acquainted with Pliny's methods of abbreviation would much rather conclude, if one must be a copyist, that his title to this office is the clearest."

From these preliminary points we pass on to consider the contents of the work, and these may be conveniently reviewed under the three heads Geography, Navigation, Commerce. In the commentary, which is to accompany the translation, the Geography will be examined in detail. Meanwhile we shall enumerate the voyages which are distinguishable in the *Periplûs*,[2] and the articles of commerce which it specifies.

---

[2] The enumeration is Vincent's, altered and abridged.

I.
VOYAGES MENTIONED IN THE PERIPLUS.

I. A voyage from *Berenîkê*, in the south of Egypt, down the western coast of the Red Sea through the Straits, along the coast of Africa, round Cape Guardafui, and then southward along the eastern coast of Africa as far as Rhapta, a place about six degrees south of the equator.

II. We are informed of two distinct courses confined to the Red Sea: one from Myos Hormos, in the south of Egypt, across the northern end of the sea to Leukê Kômê, on the opposite coast of Arabia, near the mouth of the Elanitic Gulf, whence it was continued to Mouza, an Arabian port lying not far westward from the Straits; the other from Berenîkê directly down the gulf to this same port.

III. There is described next to this a voyage from the mouth of the Straits along the southern coast of Arabia round the promontory now called Ras-el-Had, whence it was continued along the eastern coast of Arabia as far as Apologos (now Oboleh), an important emporium at the head of the Persian Gulf, near the mouth of the river Euphrates.

IV. Then follows a passage from the Straits to India by three different routes: the first by adhering to the coasts of Arabia, Karmania, Gedrosia, and Indo-Skythia, which terminated at B a r u g a z a (Bharoch), a great emporium on the river N a m m a d i o s (the Narmadâ), at a distance of thirty miles from its mouth; the second from K a n ê, a port to the west of S u a g r o s, a great projection on the south coast of Arabia, now Cape Fartaque; and the third from Cape Guardafui, on the African side—both across the ocean by the monsoon to M o u z i r i s and N e l k u n d a, great commercial cities on the coast of Malabar.

V. After this we must allow a similar voyage performed by the Indians to Arabia, or by the Arabians to India, previous to the performance of it by the Greeks, because the Greeks as late as the reign of Philomêtôr met this commerce in Sabæa.

VI. We obtain an incidental knowledge of a voyage conducted from ports on the east coast of Africa over to India by the monsoon long before Hippalos introduced the knowledge of that wind to the Roman world. This voyage was connected, no doubt, with the commerce of Arabia, since the Arabians were the great traffickers of antiquity, and held in subjection part of the sea-board of Eastern Africa. The Indian commodities imported into Africa were rice, ghee, oil of sesamum, sugar, cotton, muslins, and sashes. These commodities, the *Periplûs* informs us, were brought sometimes in vessels destined expressly for the coast of Africa, while at others they were only part of the cargo, out of vessels which were proceeding to another port. Thus we have two methods of conducting this commerce perfectly direct; and another by touching on this coast with a final destination to Arabia. This is the reason that the Greeks found cinnamon and the produce of India on this coast, when they first ventured to pass the Straits in order to seek a cheaper market than Sabæa.

II.
ARTICLES OF COMMERCE MENTIONED
IN THE PERIPLUS.

I. Animals:—

1. Παρθένοι εὐειδεῖς πρὸς παλλακίαν—Handsome girls for the haram, imported into Barugaza for the king (49).[3]

2. Δούλικα κρείσσονα—Tall slaves, procured at Opônê, imported into Egypt (14).

3. Σώματα θηλυκὰ—Female slaves, procured from Arabia and India, imported into the island of Dioskoridês (31).

4. Σώματα—Slaves imported from Omana and Apologos into Barugaza (36), and from Moundou and Malaô (8, 9).

5. Ἵπποι—Horses imported into Kanê for the king, and into Mouza for the despot (23, 24).

6. Ἡμίοναι νωτηγοί—Sumpter mules imported into Mouza for the despot (24).

II. Animal Products:—

1. Βούτυρον—Butter, or the Indian preparation therefrom called *ghî*, a product of Ariakê (41); exported from Barugaza to the Barbarine markets beyond the Straits (14). The word, according to Pliny (xxviii. 9), is of Skythian origin, though apparently connected with Βους, τυρος. The reading is, however, suspected by Lassen, who would substitute Βοσμορον or Βοσπορον, *a kind of grain*.

2. Δέρματα Σηρικὰ —Chinese hides or furs. Exported from Barbarikon, a mart on the Indus (39). Vincent suspected the reading δερματα, but groundlessly, for Pliny mentions the Sêres sending their iron along with vestments and hides (*vestibus pellibusque*), and among the presents sent to Yudhishthira by the Sâka, Tushâra and Kaṅka skins are enumerated.—*Mahâbh.* ii. 50, quoted by Lassen.

3. Ἐλέφας—Ivory. Exported from Adouli (6), Aualitês (8), Ptolemaïs (3), Mossulon (10), and the ports of Azania (16, 17). Also from Barugaza (49), Mouziris and Nelkunda (56); a species of ivory called Βωσαρη is produced in Desarênê (62).

4. Ἔριον Σηρικὸν—Chinese cotton. Imported from the country of the Thînai through Baktria to Barugaza, and by the Ganges to Bengal, and thence to Dimurikê (64). By Ἐριον Vincent seems to understand silk in the raw state.

5. Κέρατα—Horns. Exported from Barugaza to the marts of Omana and Apologos (36). Müller suspects this reading, thinking it strange that such an article as *horns* should be mentioned between *wooden beams* and *logs*. He thinks, therefore, that Κέρατα is either used in some technical sense, or that the reading Κορμῶν or Κορμίων should be substituted—adding that Κορμοὺς ἐβένου, *planks of ebony*, are at all events mentioned by Athênaios (p. 201*a*) where he is quoting Kallixenos of

---

[3] The numerals indicate the sections of the *Periplûs* in which the articles are mentioned.

Rhodes.

6. Κοράλλιον—Coral. (Sans. *pravâla*, Hindi *mûngâ*.) Imported into Kanê (28), Barbarikon on the Indus (39), Barugaza (49), and Naoura, Tundis, Mouziris, and Nelkunda (56).

7. Λάκκος χρωμάτινος—Coloured lac. Exported to Adouli from Ariakê (6). The Sanskrit word is *lâkshâ*, which is probably a later form of *râkshâ*, connected, as Lassen thinks, with *râga*, from the root *rańj*, to dye. The vulgar form is *lâkkha*. Gum-lac is a substance produced on the leaves and branches of certain trees by an insect, both as a covering for its egg and food for its young. It yields a fine red dye.[4] Salmasius thinks that by λάκκος χρωμάτινος must be understood not lac itself, but vestments dyed therewith.

8. Μαργαρίτης—Pearl. (Sans. *mukta*, Hindi, *motí*.) Exported in considerable quantity and of superior quality from Mouziris and Nelkunda (56). Cf. πινικον.

9. Νημα Σηρικόν—Silk thread. From the country of the Thînai: imported into Barugaza and the marts of Dimurikê (64). Exported from Barugaza (49), and also from Barbarikon on the Indus (39)." It is called μέταξα by Procopius and all the later writers, as well as by the *Digest*, and was known without either name to Pliny"—Vincent.

10. Πινίκιος κόγχος—the Pearl-oyster. (Sans. *śukti*.) Fished for at the entrance to the Persian Gulf (35). Pearl πίνικον inferior to the Indian sort exported in great quantity from the marts of Apologos and Omana (36). A pearl fishery (Πινικοῦ κολύμβησις) in the neighbourhood of Kolkhoi, in the kingdom of Pandiôn, near the island of Epiodôros; the produce transported to Argalou, in the interior of the country, where muslin robes with pearl inwoven (μαργαρίτιδες σινδόνες) were fabricated (59). The reading of the MS. is σινδόνες, ἐβαργαρείτιδες λεγόμεναι, for which Salmasius proposed to read μαργαριτιδες. Müller suggests instead αἱ Ἀργαρίτιδες, as if the muslin bore the name of the place *Argarou* or *Argulou*, where it was made.

Pearl is also obtained in Taprobanê (61); is imported into the emporium on the Ganges called Gangê (63).

11. Πορφύρα—Purple. Of a common as well as of a superior quality, imported from Egypt into Mouza (24) and Kanê (28), and from the marts of Apologos and Omana into Barugaza (36).

12. Ῥινόκερως—Rhinoceros (Sans. *khadgaḍ*)—the horn or the teeth, and probably the skin. Exported from Adouli (16), and the marts of Azania (7). Bruce found the hunting of the rhinoceros still a trade in Abyssinia.

13. Χελώνη—Tortoise (Sans. *kachchhapa*) or tortoise-shell. Exported from Adouli (6) and Aualitês (7); a small quantity of the genuine and land tortoise,

---

[4] Bhagvânlâl Indraji Pâṇḍit points out that the colour is called *alaktaka*, Prakrit *alito*: it is used by women for dying the nails and feet,—also as a dye. The *gulalî* or pill-like balls used by women are made with arrowroot coloured with *alito*, and cotton dipped in it is sold in the bazars under the name of *pothi*, and used for the same purposes. He has also contributed many of the Sanskrit names, and some notes.

and a white sort with a small shell, exported from Ptolemaïs (3); small shells (Χελωνάρια) exported from Mossulon (10); a superior sort in great quantity from Opônê (13); the mountain tortoise from the island of Menouthias (15); a kind next in quality to the Indian from the marts of Azania (16, 17); the genuine, land, white, and mountain sort with shells of extraordinary size from the island of Dioskoridês (30, 31); a good quantity from the island of Serapis (33); the best kind in all the Erythræan—that of the Golden Khersonêsos (63), sent to Mouziris and Nelkunda, whence it is exported along with that of the islands off the coast of Dimurikê (probably the Laccadive islands) (56); tortoise is also procured in Taprobanê (61).

III.—Plants and their products:—

1. Ἀλόη—the aloe (Sans. *agaru*). Exported from Kanê (28). The sort referred to is probably the bitter cathartic, not the aromatic sort supposed by some to be the sandalwood. It grows abundantly in Sokotra, and it was no doubt exported thence to Kanê. "It is remarkable," says Vincent, "that when the author of the *Periplûs* arrives at Sokotra he says nothing of the aloe, and mentions only Indian cinnabar as a gum or resin distilling from a tree: but the confounding of cinnabar with dragon's-blood was a mistake of ancient date and a great absurdity" (II. p. 689).

2. Ἀρώματα—aromatics (ευωδια, θυμιαματα.) Exported from Aualitês (7), Mossulon (10). Among the spices of Tabai (12) are enumerated ἀσύβη καί ἄρωμα καί μάγλα, and similarly among the commodities of Opônê κασσία καὶ ἄρωμα καὶ μότω; and in these passages perhaps a particular kind of aromatic (cinnamon?) may by preëminence be called ἄρωμα. The occurrence, however, in two instances of such a familiar word as ἄρωμα between two outlandish words is suspicious, and this has led Müller to conjecture that the proper reading may be ἀρηβώ, which Salmasius, citing Galen, notes to be a kind of cassia.

3. Ασύβη—Asuphê, a kind of cassia. Exported from Tabai (12). "This term," says Vincent, "if not Oriental, is from the Greek ἀσύφηλος, signifying *cheap* or *ordinary*; but we do not find ἀσύφη used in this manner by other authors: it may be an Alexandrian corruption of the language, or it may be the abbreviation of a merchant in his invoice." (*Asafœtida*, Sans. *hingu* or *bâhlika*, Mar. *hing*.)

4. Βδελλα, (common form Βδελλιον). Bdella, Bdellium, produced on the sea-coast of Gedrosia (37); exported from Barbarikon on the Indus (39); brought from the interior of India to Barugaza (48) for foreign export (49). Bdella is the gum of the *Balsamodendron Mukul*, a tree growing in Sind, Kâthiâvâḍ, and the Dîsâ district.[5] It is used both as an incense and as a cordial medicine. The bdellium of Scripture is a crystal, and has nothing in common with the bdellium of the *Periplûs* but its transparency. Conf. Dioskorid. i. 80; Plin. xii. 9; Galen, *Therapeut. ad Glauc.* II. p. 106; Lassen, *Ind. Alt.* vol. I. p. 290; Vincent, vol. II. p. 690; Yule's *Marco Polo*, vol. II. p. 387. The etymology of the word is uncertain. Lassen suspects it to be Indian.

5. Γίζειρ—Gizeir, a kind of cassia exported from Tabai (12). This sort is noticed and described by Dioskoridês.

6. Δόκος—Beams of wood. Exported from Barugaza to the marts of Omana

[5] Sans. *Guggula*, Guj. *Gûgal*, used as a tonic and for skin and urinary diseases.—B. I. P.

and Apologos (36). (? Blackwood.)

7. Δούακα—Douaka, a kind of cassia. Exported from Malaô and Moundou (8, 9). It was probably that inferior species which in Dioskorid. i. 12, is called δακαϱ or δακαϱ or δαϱκα.

8. Ἐβένιναι φάλαγγες—Logs of ebony (*Diospyros melanoxylon.*) Exported from Barugaza to the marts of Omana and Apologos (36).

9. Ελαιον—Oil (*tila*). Exported from Egypt to Adouli (6); ἔλαιον σησαμινον, oil of sêsamê, a product of Ariakê (41). Exported from Barugaza to the Barbarine markets (14), and to Moskha in Arabia (32).[6]

10. Ἰνδικόν μέλαν—Indigo. (Sans. *nîlî*, Guj. *gulî*.) Exported from Skythic Barbarikon (39). It appears pretty certain that the culture of the indigo plant and the preparation of the drug have been practised in India from a very remote epoch. It has been questioned, indeed, whether the Indicum mentioned by Pliny (xxxv. 6) was indigo, but, as it would seem, without any good reason. He states that it was brought from India, and that when diluted it produced an admirable mixture of blue and purple colours. *Vide* McCulloch's *Commer. Dict.* s. v. *Indigo.* Cf. Salmas, in *Exerc.* Plin. p. 181. The dye was introduced into Rome only a little before Pliny's time.

11. Κάγκαμον—Kankamon. Exported from Malaô and Moundou (8, 10). According to Dioskoridês i. 23, it is the exudation of a wood, like myrrh, and used for fumigation. Cf. Plin. xii. 44. According to Scaliger it was gum-lac used as a dye. It is the "dekamalli" gum of the bazars.

12. Κάϱπασος—Karpasus (Sans. *kârpâsa'*; Heb. karpas,) *Gossypium arboreum*, fine muslin—a product of Ariakê (41). "How this word found its way into Italy, and became the Latin *carbasus*, fine linen, is surprising, when it is not found in the Greek language. The Καϱπασιον λινον of Pausanias (*in Atticis*), of which the wick was formed for the lamp of Pallas, is asbestos, so called from Karpasos, a city of Crete—Salmas. Plin. *Exercit.* p. 178. Conf. Q. Curtius viii. 9:—'Carbaso Indi corpora usque ad pedes velant, corumque rex lecticâ margaritis circumpendentibus recumbit distinctis auro et purpurâ carbasis quâ indutus est.'" Vincent II. 699.

13. Κασσία or Κασία (Sans. *kuta*, Heb. *kiddah* and *keziah*). Exported from Tabai (12); a coarse kind exported from Malaô and Moundou (8, 9); a vast quantity exported from Mossulon and Opônê (10, 13).

"This spice," says Vincent, "is mentioned frequently in the *Periplûs*, and with various additions, intended to specify the different sorts, properties, or appearances of the commodity. It is a species of cinnamon, and manifestly the same as what we call cinnamon at this day; but different from that of the Greeks and Romans, which was not a bark, nor rolled up into pipes, like ours. Theirs was the tender shoot of the same plant, and of much higher value." "If our cinnamon," he adds, "is the ancient casia, our casia again is an inferior sort of cinnamon." Pliny (xii. 19) states that the cassia is of a larger size than the cinnamon, and has a thin rind rather than a bark, and that its value consists in being hollowed out. Dioskoridês

---

[6] Mahuwâ oil (Guj. *doliuṅ*, Sans. *madhuka*) is much exported from Bharoch.—B. I. P.

mentions cassia as a product of Arabia, but this is a mistake, Arabian cassia having been an import from India. Herodotos (iii.) had made the same mistake, saying that cassia grew in Arabia, but that cinnamon was brought thither by birds from the country where Bacchus was born (India). The cassia shrub is a sort of laurel. There are ten kinds of cassia specified in the *Periplûs*.[7] Cf. Lassen, *Ind. Alt.* I. 279, 283; Salmas. Plin. *Exercit.* p. 1304; Galen, *de Antidotis*, bk. i.

14. Κιννάβαρι Ἰνδικὸν—Dragon's-blood, *damu'l akhawein* of the Arabs, a gum distilled from *Pterocarpus Draco*, a leguminous tree[8] in the island of Dioskoridês or Sokotra (30). Cinnabar, with which this was confounded, is the red sulphuret of mercury. Pliny (lib. xxix. c. 8) distinguishes it as 'Indian cinnabar.' Dragon's-blood is one of the concrete balsams, the produce of *Calamus Draco*, a species of rattan palm of the Eastern Archipelago, [of *Pterocarpus Draco*, allied to the Indian Kino tree or *Pt. marsupium* of South India, and of *Dracæna Draco*, a liliaceous tree of Madeira and the Canary Islands].

15. Κόστος (Sansk. *kushṭa*, Mar. *choka*, Guj. *kaṭha* and *pushkara mûla*,)—Kostus. Exported from Barbarikon, a mart on the Indus (39), and from Barugaza, which procured it from Kâbul through Proklaïs, &c. This was considered the best of aromatic roots, as nard or spikenard was the best of aromatic plants. Pliny (xii. 25) describes this root as hot to the taste and of consummate fragrance, noting that it was found at the head of Patalênê, where the Indus bifurcates to form the Delta, and that it was of two sorts, black and white, black being of an inferior quality. Lassen states that two kinds are found in India—one in Multân, and the other in Kâbul and Kâśmîr. "The Costus of the ancients is still exported from Western India, as well as from Calcutta to China, under the name of *Putchok*, to be burnt as an incense in Chinese temples. Its identity has been ascertained in our own days by Drs. Royle and Falconer as the root of a plant which they called *Aucklandia Costus*.... Alexander Hamilton, at the beginning of last century, calls it *ligna dulcis* (sic), and speaks of it as an export from Sind, as did the author of the *Periplûs* 1600 years earlier." Yule's *Marco Polo*, vol. II. p. 388.

16. Κρόκος—Crocus, Saffron. (Sans. *kaśmîraja*, Guj. *kesir*, Pers. *zafrân*.) Exported from Egypt to Mouza (24) and to Kanê (28).

17. Κύπερος—Cyprus. Exported from Egypt to Mouza (24). It is an aromatic rush used in medicine (Pliny xxi. 18). Herodotos (iv. 71) describes it as an aromatic plant used by the Skythians for embalming. Κύπερος is probably Ionic for Κύπειρος—Κύπειρος ἰνδικὸς of Dioskoridês, and *Cypria herba indica* of Pliny.— Perhaps Turmeric, *Curcuma longa*, or Galingal possibly.

18. Λέντια, (Lat. *lintea*)—Linen. Exported from Egypt to Adouli (6).

19. Λίβανος (Heb. *lebonah*, Arab. *luban*, Sans. *śrîvâsa*)—Frankincense. Peratic or Libyan frankincense exported from the Barbarine markets—Tabai (12), Mossulon (10), Malaô and Moundou, in small quantities (8, 9); produced in great abundance

---

[7] May not some of these be the fragrant root of the kusâ, grass, *Andropogon calamus—aromaticus?*—J. B.

[8] A similar gum is obtained from the *Pâlâśa* (Guj. *khâkhara*), the *Dhâka* of Râjputâna.—B. I. P.

and of the best quality at Akannai (11); Arabian frankincense exported from Kanê (28). A magazine for frankincense on the Sakhalitic Gulf near Cape Suagros (30). Moskha, the port whence it was shipped for Kanê and India (32) and Indo-Skythia (39).

Regarding this important product Yule thus writes:—"The coast of Hadhramaut is the true and ancient Χώρα λιβανοφόρος or λιβανωτοφόρος, indicated or described under those names by Theophrastus, Ptolemy, Pliny, Pseudo-Arrian, and other classical writers, *i.e.* the country producing the fragrant gum-resin called by the Hebrews *Lebonah*, by the Arabs *Luban* and *Kundur*, by the Greeks *Libanos*, by the Romans *Thus*, in mediæval Latin *Olibanum* (probably the Arabic *al-luban*, but popularly interpreted as *oleum Libani*), and in English frankincense, *i.e*, I apprehend, 'genuine incense' or 'incense proper.'[9] It is still produced in this region and exported from it, but the larger part of that which enters the markets of the world is exported from the roadsteads of the opposite Sumâlî coast. Frankincense when it first exudes is milky white; whence the name *white incense* by which Polo speaks of it, and the Arabic name *luban* apparently refers to milk. The elder Niebuhr, who travelled in Arabia, depreciated the Libanos of Arabia, representing it as greatly inferior to that brought from India, called Benzoin. He adds that the plant which produces it is not native, but originally from Abyssinia."—*Marco Polo*, vol. II. p. 443, &c.

20. Λύκιον—Lycium. Exported from Barbarikon in Indo-Skythia (39), and from Barugaza (49). Lycium is a thorny plant, so called from being found in Lykia principally. Its juice was used for dying yellow, and a liquor drawn from it was used as a medicine (Celsus v. 26, 30, and vi. 7). It was held in great esteem by the ancients. Pliny (xxiv. 77) says that a superior kind of Lycium produced in India was made from a thorn called also *Pyxacanthus* (box-thorn) *Chironia*. It is known in India as *Ruzot*, an extract of the *Berberis lycium* and *B. aristata*, both grown on the Himâlayas. Conf. the λύκιον ἰνδικὸν of Dioskor. i. 133. (? Gamboge.)

21. Μάγλα—Magla—a kind of cassia mentioned only in the *Periplûs*. Exported from Tabai (12).

22. Μάκειρ—Macer. Exported from Malaô and Moundou (8, 9). According to Pliny, Dioskoridês, and others, it is an Indian bark—perhaps a kind of cassia. The bark is red and the root large. The bark was used as a medicine in dysenteries. Pliny xii. 8; Salmasius, 1302. (? The *Karachâlâ* of the bâzârs, *Kutajatvak*).

23. Μάλαβαθρον (Sans. *tamâlapattra*, the leaf of the *Laurus Cassia*), Malabathrum, Betel. Obtained by the Thînai from the Sesatai and exported to India[10] (65); conveyed down the Ganges to Gangê near its mouth (63); conveyed from the interior of India to Mouziris and Nelkunda for export (56). That Malabathrum was not only a masticatory, but also an unguent or perfume, may be inferred from Horace (*Odes*, II. vii. 89):—

... "coronatus nitentes

---

[9] What the Brâhmans call *kuṇḍaru* is the gum of a tree called the *Dhûpa-salai;* another sort of it, from Arabia, they call *Isêsa*, and in Kâṭhiâvâḍ it is known as *Sesagundar*.—B. I. P.

[10] More likely from Nepâl, where it is called *tejapât*.—B. I. P.

Malabathro Syrio capillos",

and from Pliny (xii. 59): "Dat et Malabathrum Syria, arborum folio convoluto, arido colore, ex quo exprimitur oleum ad unguenta: fertiliore ejusdem Egypto: laudatius tamen ex India venit." From Ptolemy (VII. ii. 16) we learn that the best Malabathrum was produced in Kirrhadia—that is, Rangpur. Dioskoridês speaks of it as a masticatory, and was aware of the confusion caused by mistaking the nard for the betel.

21. Μέλι τὸ καλάμινον, τὸ λεγομενον σάκχαρ (Sans. *śarkarâ*, Prâkṛit *sâkara*, Arab. *sukkar*, Latin *saccharum*)—Honey from canes, called Sugar. Exported from Barugaza to the marts of Barbaria (14). The first Western writer who mentions this article was Theophrastos, who continued the labours of Aristotle in natural history. He called it a sort of honey extracted from reeds. Strabo states, on the authority of Nearkhos, that reeds in India yield honey without bees. Ælian (*Hist. Anim.*) speaks of a kind of honey pressed from reeds which grow among the Prasii. Seneca (Epist. 84) speaks of sugar as a kind of honey found in India on the leaves of reeds, which had either been dropped on them from the sky as dew, or had exuded from the reeds themselves. This was a prevalent error in ancient times, *e.g.* Dioskoridês says that sugar is a sort of concreted honey found upon canes in India and Arabia Felix, and Pliny that it is collected from canes like a gum. He describes it as white and brittle between the teeth, of the size of a hazel-nut at most, and used in medicine only. So also Lucan, alluding to the Indians near the Ganges, says that they quaff sweet juices from tender reeds. Sugar, however, as is well known, must be extracted by art from the plant. It has been conjectured that the sugar described by Pliny and Dioṣkoridês was sugar candy obtained from China.

25. Μελίλωτον—Melilot, Honey-lotus. Exported from Egypt to Barugaza (49). Melilot is the Egyptian or Nymphæa Lotus, or Lily of the Nile, the stalk of which contained a sweet nutritive substance which was made into bread. So Vincent; but Melilot is a kind of clover, so called from the quantity of honey it contains. The nymphæa lotus, or what was called the Lily of the Nile, is not a true lotus, and contains no edible substance.

26. Μοκρότον. Exported from Moundou (9) and Mossulon (10). It is a sort of incense, mentioned only in the *Periplûs*.

27. Μότω—Motô—a sort of cassia exported from Tabai and Opônê (13).

28. Μύρον—Myrrh. (Sans. *bola.*) Exported from Egypt to Barugaza as a present for the king (49). It is a gum or resin issuing from a thorn found in Arabia Felix, Abyssinia, &c., *vide* σμύρνη *inf.*

29. Νάρδος (Sans. *nalada*, 'kaskas,' Heb. *nerd*) Nard, Spikenard.[11] Gangetic spikenard brought down the Ganges to Gangê, near its mouth (63), and forwarded thence to Mouziris and Nelkunda (56). Spikenard produced in the regions of the Upper Indus and in Indo-Skythia forwarded through Ozênê to Barugaza (48). Imported by the Egyptians from Barugaza and Barbarikon in Indo-Skythia (49, 39).

---

[11] Obtained from the root of *Nardostachys jatamansi*, a native of the eastern Himâlayas.—J. B.

The *Nardos* is a plant called (from its root being shaped like an ear of corn) νάρδου στάχυς, also ναρδόσταχυς, Latin *Spica nardi,* whence 'spikenard.' It belongs to the species *Valeriana.* "No Oriental aromatic," says Vincent, "has caused greater disputes among the critics or writers on natural history, and it is only within these few years that we have arrived at the true knowledge of this curious odour by means of the inquiries of Sir W. Jones and Dr. Roxburgh. Pliny describes the nard with its *spica,* mentioning also that both the leaves and the *spica* are of high value, and that the odour is the prime in all unguents; the price 100 denarii for a pound. But he afterwards visibly confounds it with the Malabathrum or Betel, as will appear from his usage of *Hadrosphærum, Mesosphærum,* and *Microsphærum,* terms peculiar to the Betel"—II. 743-4. See Sir W. Jones on the spikenard of the ancients in As. Res. vol. II. pp. 416 *et seq.,* and Roxburgh's additional remarks on the spikenard of the ancients, vol. IV. pp. 97 *et seq.,* and botanical observations on the spikenard, pp. 433. See also Lassen, *Ind. Alt.* vol. I. pp. 288 *et seq.*

30. Ναύπλιος—Nauplius. Exported in small quantity from the marts of Azania (17). The signification of the word is obscure, and the reading suspected. For ΝαΥΠλιος Müller suggests ΝαΡΓΙλιος, the Indian cocoanut, which the Arabians call *Nargil* (Sansk. *nârikêla* or *nâlikêra,* Guj. *nâliyêr,* Hindi *nâliyar*). It favours this suggestion that cocoanut oil is a product of Zangibar, and that in four different passages of Kosmas Indikopleustês nuts are called αργελλια, which is either a corrupt reading for ναργελλια, or Kosmas may not have known the name accurately enough.

31. Ὀθόνιον—Muslin. Sêric muslin sent from the Thînai to Barugaza and Dimurikê (64). Coarse cottons produced in great quantity in Ariakê, carried down from Ozênê to Barugaza (48); large supplies sent thither from Tagara also (51); Indian muslins exported from the markets of Dimurikê to Egypt (56). Muslins of every description, Seric and dyed of a mallow colour, exported from Barugaza to Egypt (49); Indian muslin taken to the island of Dioskoridês (31); wide Indian muslins called μοναχή, *monâkhê,* i. e. of the best and finest sort; and another sort called σαγματογήνη, *sagmatogênê,* i. e. coarse cotton unfit for spinning, and used for stuffing beds, cushions, &c., exported from Barugaza to the Barbarine markets (14), and to Arabia, whence it was exported to Adouli (6). The meanings given to *monâkhê* and *sagmatogênê* (for which other readings have been suggested) are conjectural. Vincent defends the meaning assigned to *sagmatogênê* by a quotation from a passage in Strabo citing Nearkhos:—"Fine muslins are made of cotton, but the Makedonians use cotton for flocks, and stuffing of couches."

32. Οἶνος—Wine. Laodikean and Italian wine exported in small quantity to Adouli (6); to Aualitês (7), Malaê (8), Mouza (24), Kanê (28), Barbarikon in Indo-Skythia (39); the same sorts, together with Arabian wine, to Barugaza (49); sent in small quantity to Mouziris and Nelkunda (56); the region inland from Oraia bears the vine (37), which is found also in the district of Mouza (24), whence wine is exported to the marts of Azania, not for sale, but to gain the good will of the natives (17). Wine is exported also from the marts of Apologos and Omana to Barugaza (36). By Arabian wine may perhaps be meant palm or toddy wine, a great article of commerce.

33. Ὄμφακος Διοσπολιτικῆς χυλός—the juice of the sour grape of Diospolis. Exported from Egypt to Aualitês (7). This, says Vincent, was the dipse of the Orientals, and still used as a relish all over the East. *Dipse* is the rob of grapes in their unripe state, and a pleasant acid.—II. 751. This juice is called by Dioskoridês (iv. 7) in one word Ομφάκιον, and also (v. 12) Οἶνος Ὀμφακίτης. Cf. Plin. xii. 27.

34. Ὄρυζα (Sansk. *vrîhi*)—Rice. Produced in Oraia and Ariakê (37, 41), exported from Barugaza to the Barbarine markets (14), and to the island of Dioskoridês (31).

35. Πέπερι (Sansk. *pippalî,*) long pepper—Pepper. Kottonarik pepper exported in large quantities from Mouziris and Nelkunda (56); long pepper from Barugaza (49). *Kottonara* was the name of the district, and *Kottonarikon* the name of the pepper for which the district was famous. Dr. Buchanan identifies Kottonara with Kadattanâḍu, a district in the Calicut country celebrated for its pepper. Dr. Burnell, however, identifies it with Kolatta-Nâḍu, the district about Tellicherry, which, he says, is the pepper district.

36. Πυρὸς—Wheat. Exported in small quantity from Egypt to Kanê (28), some grown in the district around Mouza (24).

37. Σάκχαρι—Sugar: see under Μελι.

38. Σανδαράκη—Sandarakê (*chandrasa* of the bazars); a resin from the *Thuja articulata* or *Callitris quadrivalvis*, a small coniferous tree of North Africa; it is of a faint aromatic smell and is used as incense. Exported from Egypt to Barugaza (49); conveyed to Mouziris and Nelkunda (56).[12]

Sandarakê also is a red pigment—red sulphuret of arsenic, as orpiment is the yellow sulphuret. Cf. Plin. xxxv. 22, Hard. "Juba informs us that sandarace and ochre are found in an island of the Red Sea, Topazas, whence they are brought to us."

39. Σαντάλινα and σασάμινα ξύλα—Logs of Sandal and Sasame (*santalum album*). Exported from Barugaza to the marts of Omana and Apologos (30). Σαντάλινα is a correction of the MS. reading τρόχιος proposed by Salmasius. Kosmas Indikopleustes calls sandalwood τζαδάνα. For σασαμινα of the MS. Stuckius proposed σησάμινα—a futile, emendation, since sesame is known only as a leguminous plant from which an oil is expressed, and not as a tree. But possibly Red Saunders wood (*Pterocarpus Santalinus*) may be meant.

40. Σησάμινον ἔλαιον. See Ελαιον.

41. Σινδόνες διαφορώτατατ αἱ Γαγγητικᾱι. The finest Bengal muslins exported from the Ganges (63); other muslins in Taprobanê (61); Μαργαριτιδες (?), made at Argalou and thence exported (59); muslins of all sorts and mallow-tinted (μολοχιναι) sent from Ozênê to Barugaza (48), exported thence to Arabia for the supply of the market at Adouli (6).

42. Σῖτος—Corn. Exported from Egypt to Adouli (7), Malaô (8); a little to Mouza (24), and to Kanê (28), and to Muziris and Nelkunda for ships' stores (56); exported from Dimurikê and Ariakê into the Barbarine markets (14), into Moskha

[12] It is brought now from the Eastern Archipelago.—B. I. P.

(32) and the island of Dioskoridês (31); exported also from Mouza to the ports of Azania for presents (17).

43. Σμύρνη—Myrrh (vide μυρον). Exported from Malaô, Moundou, Mossulon (8, 9, 10); from Aualitês a small quantity of the best quality (7); a choice sort that trickles in drops, called *Abeirminaia* (ἐκλεκτὴ καὶ στακτὴ ἀβειρμιναία), exported from Mouza (24). For Ἀβειρμιναία of the MS. Müller suggests to read γαβειρμιναία, inclining to think that two kinds of myrrh are indicated, the names of which have been erroneously combined into one, viz. the Gabiræan and Minæan, which are mentioned by Dioskoridês, Hippokratês, and Galen. There is a *Wadi Gabir* in Oman.

44. Στύραξ—Storax (Sans. *turuska, selarasa* of the bazars),—one of the balsams. Exported from Egypt to Kanê (28), Barbarikon on the Indus (39), Barugaza (40). Storax is the produce of the tree *Liquidambar orientale*, which grows in the south of Europe and the Levant.[13] The purest kind is storax in grains. Another kind is called *styrax calamita*, from being brought in masses wrapped up in the leaves of a certain reed. Another kind, that sold in shops, is semi-fluid.

45. Φοῖνιξ—the Palm or Dates. Exported from the marts of Apologos and Omana to Barugaza (36, 37).

IV.—Metals and Metallic Articles:—

1. Ἀργυρᾶ σκεύη, ἀργυρώματα—Vessels of silver. Exported from Egypt to Mossulon (10), to Barbarikon on the Indus (39). Silver plate chased or polished (τορνευτα or τετορνευμενα) sent as presents to the despot of Mouza (24), to Kanê for the king (28). Costly (βαρυτιμα) plate to Barugaza for the king (49). Plate made according to the Egyptian fashion to Adouli for the king (6).

2. Ἀρσενικὸν—Arsenic (*somal*). Exported from Egypt to Mouziris and Nelkunda (56).

3. Δηνάριον—Denary. Exported in small quantity from Egypt to Adouli (6). Gold and silver denarii sent in small quantity to the marts of Barbaria (8, 13); exchanges with advantage for native money at Barugaza (49).

The *denary* was a Roman coin equal to about 8½*d.*, and a little inferior in value to the Greek drachma.

4. Κάλτις—Kaltis. A gold coin (νομισμα) current in the district of the Lower Ganges (63); Benfey thinks the word is connected with the Sanskrit *kalita*, i.e. *numeratum*.

5. Κασσίτερος (Sans. *banga, kathila*)—Tin. Exported from Egypt to Aualitês (7), Malaô (8), Kanê (28), Barugaza (49), Mouziris and Nelkunda (56). India produced this metal, but not in those parts to which the Egyptian trade carried it.

6. Μόλυβδος—Lead (Sansk. *nâga*, Guj. *sîsun*). Exported from Egypt to Barugaza, Muziris, and Nelkunda (49, 56).

7. Ὀρείχαλκος—Orichalcum (Sans. *tripus*, Prak. *pîtala*)—Brass. Used for orna-

---

[13] In early times it was obtained chiefly from *Styrax officinalis*, a native of the same region.—J. B.

ments and cut into small pieces by way of coin. Exported from Egypt to Adouli (6).

The word means 'mountain copper.' Ramusio calls it white copper from which the gold and silver have not been well separated in extracting it from the ore. Gold, it may be remarked, does not occur as an export from any of the African marts, throughout the *Periplûs*.

8. Σίδηρος, σιδηρύ σκεύη—Iron, iron utensils. Exported from Egypt to Malaô, Moundou, Tabai, Opônê (8, 9, 12, 13). Iron spears, swords and adzes exported to Adouli (6). Indian iron and sword-blades (στομωμα) exported to Adouli from Arabia (Ariakê?). Spears (λόγχαι) manufactured at Mouza, hatchets (πελύκια), swords (μάχαιραι), awls (ὀπέτια) exported from Mouza to Azania (17).

On the Indian sword see Ktêsias, p. 80, 4. The Arabian poets celebrate swords made of Indian steel. Cf. Plin. xxxiv. 41:—"Ex omnibus autem generibus palma Serico ferro est." This iron, as has already been stated, was sent to India along with skins and cloth. Cf. also Edrisi, vol. I. p. 65, ed. Joubert. Indian iron is mentioned in the Pandects as an article of commerce.

9. Στίμμι—Stibium (Sans. *sauvîrânjana*, Prâk. *surmâ*). Exported from Egypt to Barugaza (49), to Mouziris and Nelkunda (56).

Stibium is a sulphuret of antimony, a dark pigment, called *kohol*, much used in the East for dyeing the eyelids.

10. Χαλκὸς—Copper (Sans. *tâmra*) or Brass. Exported from Egypt to Kanê (28), to Barugaza (49), Mouziris and Nelkunda (56). Vessels made thereof (Χαλκουργήματα) sent to Mouza as presents to the despot (24). Drinking-vessels (ποτηρια) exported to the marts of Barbaria (8, 13). Big and round drinking-cups to Adouli (6). A few (μελίεφθα ὀλίγα) to Malaô (8); μελίεφθα χαλκᾶ for cooking with, and being cut into bracelets and anklets for women to Adouli (6).

Regarding μελίεφθα Vincent says: "No usage of the word occurs elsewhere; but metals were prepared with several materials to give them colour, or to make them tractable, or malleable. Thus χολόβαφα in Hesychius was brass prepared with ox's gall to give it the colour of gold, and used, like our tinsel ornaments or foil, for stage dresses and decorations. Thus common brass was neither ductile nor malleable, but the Cyprian brass was both. And thus perhaps brass, μελίεφθα was formed with some preparation of honey." Müller cannot accept this view. "It is evident," he says, "that the reference is to ductile copper from which, as Pliny says, all impurity has been carefully removed by smelting, so that pots, bracelets, and articles of that sort could be fabricated from it. One might therefore think that the reading should be περίεφθα or πυρίεφθα, but in such a case the writer would have said περίεφθον χαλκόν. In vulgar speech μελίεφθα is used as a substantive noun, and I am therefore almost persuaded that, just as molten copper, ὁ χαλκὸς ὁ χυτὸς, *cuprum caldarium*, was called τρόχιος, from the likeness in shape of its round masses to hoops, so *laminæ* of ductile copper (*plaques de cuivre*) might have been called μελίεφθα, because shaped like thin honey-cakes, πεμματα μελίεφθα."

11. Χρυσὸς—Gold. Exported from the marts of Apologos and Omana to Barugaza (36). Gold plate—χρυσώματα—exported from Egypt to Mouza for the des-

pot (24), and to Adouli for the king (6).

V. Stones:—

1. Λιθία διαφανὴς—Gems (carbuncles?) found in Taprobanê (63); exported in every variety from Mouziris and Nelkunda (56).

2. Αδάμας—Diamonds. (Sans. *vajra, pîraka*). Exported from Mouziris and Nelkunda (56).

3. Καλλεανὸς λίθος—Gold-stone, yellow crystal, chrysolith? Exported from Barbarikon in Indo-Skythia (39).

It is not a settled point what stone is meant. Lassen says that the Sanskrit word *kalyâṇa* means *gold*, and would therefore identify it with the chrysolith or gold-stone. If this view be correct, the reading of the MS. need not be altered into καλλαῖνὸς, as Salmasius, whom the editors of the *Periplûs* generally follow, enjoins. In support of the alteration Salmasius adduces Pliny, xxxvii. 56:—"Callais sapphirum imitatur, candidior et litoroso mari similis. Callainas vocant e turbido Callaino", and other passages. Schwanbeck, however, maintaining the correctness of the MS. reading, says that the Sanskrit word *kalyâṇa* generally signifies *money*, but in a more general sense *anything beautiful*, and might therefore have been applied to this gem. *Kalyâṇa*, he adds, would appear in Greek as καλλιανὸς or καλλεανὸς rather than καλλαῖνὸς. In like manner *kalyâṇî* of the Indians appears in our author not as καλλάϊνα, but, as it ought to be, καλλίενα.

4. Λύγδος—Alabaster. Exported from Mouza (24). Salmasius says that an imitation of this alabaster was formed of Parian marble, but that the best and original *lygdus* was brought from Arabia, that is, Mouza, as noted in the *Periplûs*. Cf. Pliny (xxxvi. 8):—"Lygdinos in Tauro repertos ... antea ex Arabia tantum advehi solitos enndoris eximii."

5. Ὀνυχινὴ λίθια—Onyx (*akika*—agate). Sent in vast quantities (πλειστη) from Ozênê and Paithana to Barugaza (48, 51), and thence exported to Egypt (49). Regarding the onyx mines of Gujarât *vide* Ritter, vol. VI. p. 603.

6. Μουρρίνη, sup. λιθια—Fluor-spath. Sent from Ozênê to Barugaza, and exported to Egypt (49). Porcelain made at Diospolis (μουρρίνη λιθία ἡ γενομένη ἐν Διοσπόλει) exported from Egypt to Adouli (6).

The reading of the MS. is μορρίνης. By this is to be understood *vitrum murrhinum*, a sort of china or porcelain made in imitation of cups or vases of *murrha*, a precious fossil-stone resembling, if not identical with, *fluor-spath*, such as is found in Derbyshire. Vessels of this stone were exported from India, and also, as we learn from Pliny, from Karmania, to the Roman market, where they fetched extravagant prices.[14] The "cups baked in Parthian fires" (*pocula Parthis focis cocta*) mentioned by Propertius (IV. v. 26) must be referred to the former class. The whole subject is one which has much exercised the pens of the learned. "Six hundred writers," says Müller, "emulously applying themselves to explain what had the best claim to be considered the *murrha* of the ancients, have advanced the most conflicting opin-

---

[14] Nero gave for one 300 talents = £58,125. They were first seen at Rome in the triumphal procession of Pompey. [May these not have been of emerald, or even ruby?—J. B.]

ions. Now it is pretty well settled that the murrhine vases were made of that stone which is called in German *flusspath (spato-fluore)*". He then refers to the following as the principal authorities on the subject:—Pliny—xxxiii. 7 *et seq.*; xxxiii. *proœm.* Suetonius—*Oct.* c. 71; Seneca—*Epist.* 123; Martial—iv. 86; xiv. 43; *Digest*—xxxiii. 10, 3; xxxiv. 2. 19; Rozière—*Mémoire sur les Vases murrhins*, &c.; in *Description de l'Égypt*, vol. VI. pp. 277 *et seq.*: Corsi—*Delle Pietre antiche*, p. 106; Thiersch—*Ueber die Vasa Murrhina der Alten, in Abhandl. d. Munchn. Akad.* 1835, vol. I. pp. 443-509; A learned Englishman in the *Classical Journal* for 1810, p. 472; Witzsch in Pauly's *Real Encycl.* vol. V. p. 253. See also Vincent, vol. II. pp. 723-7.

7. Ὀψιανὸς λίθος—the Opsian or Obsidian stone, found in the Bay of Hanfelah (5). Pliny says,—"The opsians or obsidians are also reckoned as a sort of glass bearing the likeness of the stone which Obsius (or Obsidius) found in Ethiopia, of a very black colour, sometimes even translucent, hazier than ordinary glass to look through, and when used for mirrors on the walls reflecting but shadows instead of distinct images." (Bk. xxxvi. 37). The only Obsius mentioned in history is a M. Obsius who had been Prætor, a friend of Germanicus, referred to by Tacitus (*Ann.* IV. 68, 71). He had perhaps been for a time prefect of Egypt, and had coasted the shore of Ethiopia at the time when Germanicus traversed Egypt till he came to the confines of Ethiopia. Perhaps, however, the name of the substance is of Greek origin—ὀψιανὸς, from its reflecting power.

8. Σάπφειρος—the Sapphire. Exported from Barbarikon in Indo-Skythia (39). "The ancients distinguished two sorts of dark blue or purple, one of which was spotted with gold. Pliny says it is never pellucid, which seems to make it a different stone from what is now called sapphire."—Vincent (vol. II. p. 757), who adds in a note, "Dr. Burgess has specimens of both sorts, the one with gold spots like lapis lazuli, and not transparent."[15]

9. Ὑάκινθος—Hyacinth or Jacinth. Exported from Mouziris and Nelkunda (56). According to Salmasius this is the Ruby. In Solinus xxx. it would seem to be the Amethyst (Sansk. *pushkarâja.*)

10. Ὕαλος ἀργὴ—Glass of a coarse kind. Exported from Egypt to Barugaza (49), to Mouziris and Nelkunda (56). Vessels of glass (ὕαλα σκευη) exported from Egypt to Barbarikon in Indo-Skythia (39). Crystal of many sorts (λιθίας ὑαλῆς πλεῖστα γενη) exported from Egypt to Adouli, Aualitês, Mossulon (6, 7, 10); from Mouza to Azania (17).

11. Χρυσόλιθος—Chrysolite. Exported from Egypt to Barbarikon in Indo-Skythia (39), to Barugaza (43), to Mouziris and Nelkunda (56). Some take this to be the topaz (Hind. *pîrojâ*).

VI. Wearing Apparel:—

1. Ἱμάτια ἄγναφα—Cloths undressed. Manufactured in Egypt and thence exported to Adouli (6). These were disposed of to the tribes of Barbaria—the Troglodyte shepherds of Upper Egypt, Nubia and Ethiopia.

2. Ἱμάτια βαρβαρικὰ σύμμικτα γεγναμμένα—Cloths for the Barbarine mar-

---

[15] Possibly the Lapis Lazuli is meant.—J. B.

kets, dressed and dyed of various colours. Exported to Malaô and Aualitês (8, 7).

3. Ἱματισμὸς Ἀραβικὸς—Cloth or coating for the Arabian markets. Exported from Egypt (24). Different kinds are enumerated:—Χειριδωτὸς, with sleeves reaching to the wrist; Ὁτε ἁπλοῦς καὶ ὁ κοινὸς, with single texture and of the common sort; σκοτουλάτος, wrought with figures, checkered; the word is a transliteration of the Latin *scutulatus*, from *scutum*, the checks being lozenge-shaped, like a shield: see Juvenal, Sat. ii. 79; διάχρυσος, shot with gold; πολυτελὴς, a kind of great price sent to the despot of Mouza; Κοινὸς καὶ ἁπλοῦς καὶ ὁ νόθος, cloth of a common sort, and cloth of simple texture, and cloth in imitation of a better commodity, sent to Kanê (28); Διάφορος ἁπλους, of superior quality and single texture, for the king (28); Ἁπλοῦς, *of single texture*, in great quantity, and νόθος, in inferior sort imitating a better, in small quantity, sent to Barbarikon in Indo-Skythia (39), ἁπλοῦς καὶ νόθος παντοῖος, and for the king ἁπλοῦς πολυτελης, sent to Barugaza (49); Ἱματισμὸς οὐ πολύς—cloth in small quantity sent to Muziris and Nelkunda (56); ἐντόπιος, of native manufacture, exported from the marts of Apologos and Omana to Barugaza (36).

4. Αβόλλαι—Riding or watch cloaks. Exported from Egypt to Mouza (34), to Kanê (28). This word is a transliteration of the Latin *Abolla*. It is supposed, however, to be derived from Greek: ἀμβολλη, i. e. ἀμφιβολὴ. It was a woollen cloak of close texture—often mentioned in the Roman writers: *e.g.* Juven. *Sat.* iii. 115 and iv. 70; Sueton. *Calig.* c. 35. Where the word occurs in sec. 6 the reading of the MS. is ἄβολοι, which Müller has corrected to ἀβόλλαι, though Salmasius had defended the original reading.

5. Δικρόσσια (Lat. *Mantilia utrinque fimbriata*)—Cloths with a double fringe. Exported from Egypt to Adouli (6). This word occurs only in the *Periplûs*. The simple Κροσσιον, however, is met with in Herodian, *Epim.* p. 72. An adjective δίκροσσος is found in Pollux vii. 72. "We cannot err much," says Vincent, "in rendering the δικρόσσια of the *Periplûs* either *cloth fringed*, with Salmasius, or *striped*, with Apollonius. Meursius says λεντία ἄκροσσα are *plain linens not striped.*"

6. Ζῶναι πολύμιτοι πηχυαῖοι—Flowered or embroidered girdles, a cubit broad. Exported from Egypt to Barugaza (49). Σκιωταὶ—girdles (*kâcha*) shaded of different colours, exported to Mouza (24). This word occurs only in the *Periplûs*.

7. Καυνάκαὶ—Garments of frieze. Exported from Arabia to Adouli (6); a pure sort—ἁπλοι—exported to the same mart from Egypt (6). In the latter of these two passages the MS. reading is γαυνάκαὶ. Both forms are in use: conf. Latin *gaunace*—Varro, *de L. L.* 4, 35. It means also *a fur garment* or *blanket*—*vestis stragula.*

8. Λώδικες—Quilts or coverlids. Exported in small quantity from Egypt to Mouza (24) and Kanê (28).

9. Περιζώματα—Sashes, girdles, or aprons. Exported from Barugaza to Adouli (6), and into Barbaria (14).

10. Πολύμιτα—Stuffs in which several threads were taken for the woof in order to weave flowers or other objects: Latin *polymita* and *plumatica*. Exported from Egypt to Barbarikon in Indo-Skythia (39), to Mouziris and Nelkunda (56).

11. Σάγοι Ἀρσινοητικοὶ γεγναμμένοι καὶ βεβαμμένοι—Coarse cloaks made at Arsinoê, dressed and dyed. Exported from Egypt to Barbaria (8, 13).

12. Στολαὶ Ἀρσινοητικάι—Women's robes made at Arsinoê. Exported from Egypt to Adouli (6).

13. Χιτῶνες—Tunics. Exported from Egypt to Malaô, Moundou, Mossulon (8, 9, 10).

VII. In addition to the above, works of art are mentioned.

Ἀνδριάντες—Images, sent as presents to Kharibaël (48). Cf. Strabo (p. 714), who among the articles sent to Arabia enumerates τορευμα, γραφην, πλασμα, pieces of sculpture, painting, statues.

Μουσικά—Instruments of music, for presents to the king of Ariakê (49).

ANONYMI [ARRIANI UT FERTUR] PERIPLUS MARIS ERYTHRÆI.

1. The first of the important roadsteads established on the Red Sea, and the first also of the great trading marts upon its coast, is the port of M y o s - h o r m o s in Egypt. Beyond it at a distance of 1800 stadia is B e r e n i k ê, which is to your right if you approach it by sea. These roadsteads are both situate at the furthest end of Egypt, and are bays of the Red Sea.

Commentary.

(1) *M y o s   H o r m o s.* —Its situation is determined by the cluster of islands now called *J i f â t î n* [lat. 27° 12′ N., long. 33° 55′ E.] of which the three largest lie opposite an indenture of the coast of Egypt on the curve of which its harbour was situated [near Ras Abu Somer, a little north of Satâjah Island]. It was founded by Ptolemy Philadelphos B. C. 274, who selected it as the principal port of the Egyptian trade with India in preference to Arsinoê,[16] N. N. E. of Suez, on account of the difficulty and tediousness of the navigation down the Heroöpolite Gulf. The vessels bound for Africa and the south of Arabia left its harbour about the time of the autumnal equinox, when the North West wind which then prevailed carried them quickly down the Gulf. Those bound for the Malabar Coast or Ceylon left in July, and if they cleared the Red Sea before the 1st of September, they had the monsoon to assist their passage across the ocean. *M y o s   H o r m o s* was distant from *K o p - t o s* [lat. 26° N.], the station on the Nile through which it communicated with Alexandria, a journey of seven or eight days along a road opened through the desert by Philadelphos. The name *M y o s   H o r m o s* is of Greek origin, and may signify either the Harbour of the Mouse, or, more probably, of the Mussel, since the pearl mussel abounded in its neighbourhood. *A g a t h a r k h i d ê s* calls it *A p h r o d i t ē s   H o r m o s,* and Pliny *V e n e r i s   P o r t u s.* [Veneris Portus however was probably at Sherm Sheikh, lat. 24° 36′ N. Off the coast is Wade Jemâl Island, lat. 24° 39′ N., long. 35° 8′ E., called Iambe by Pliny, and perhaps the Aphroditês Island of Ptolemy IV. v. 77.] Referring to this name Vincent says: "Here

---

[16] There was another Arsinoe between Ras Dh'ib and Ras Shukhair, lat. 28° 3′ N. The few geographical indications added by Mr. Burgess to these comments as they passed through the press are enclosed in brackets. [ ]

if the reader will advert to Aphroditê, the Greek title of Venus, as springing from the foam of the ocean, it will immediately appear that the Greeks were translating here, for the native term to this day is *Suffange-el-Bahri*, 'sponge of the sea'; and the vulgar error of the sponge being the foam of the sea, will immediately account for Aphroditê."

The rival of Myos-Hormos was *Berenikê*, a city built by Ptolemy Philadelphos, who so named it in honour of his mother, who was the daughter of Ptolemy Lagos and Antigonê. It was in the same parallel with Syênê and therefore not far from the Tropic [lat. 23° 55′ N.]. It stood nearly at the bottom of *Foul Bay* (ἐν βάθει τοῦ Ἀκαθάρτου so Κὸλπου), called from the coast being foul with shoals and breakers, and not from the impurity of its water, as its Latin name, *Sinus Immundus*, would lead us to suppose. Its ruins are still perceptible even to the arrangement of the streets, and in the centre is a small Egyptian temple adorned with hieroglyphics and bas-reliefs of Greek workmanship. Opposite to the town is a very fine natural harbour, the entrance of which has been deep enough for small vessels, though the bar is now impassable at low water. Its prosperity under the Ptolemies and afterwards under the Romans was owing to its safe anchorage and its being, like Myos-Hormos, the terminus of a great road from Koptos along which the traffic of Alexandria with Ethiopia, Arabia, and India passed to and fro. Its distance from *Koptos* was 258 Roman miles or 11 days' journey. The distance between Myos-Hormos and Berenikê is given in the *Periplûs* at 225 miles, but this is considerably above the mark. The difficulty of the navigation may probably have made the distance seem greater than it was in reality.

2. The country which adjoins them on the right below Berenîkê is B a r b a r i a . Here the sea-board is peopled by the I k h t h y o p h a g o i , who live in scattered huts built in the narrow gorges of the hills, and further inland are the B e r b e r s , and beyond them the A g r i o p h a g o i and M o s k h o p h a g o i , tribes under regular government by kings. Beyond these again, and still further inland towards the west [is situated the metropolis called Meroê].

(2) Adjoining *Berenikê* was *Barbaria* (ἡ Βαρβαρικὴ χώρα)—the land about Ras Abû Fatima [lat. 22° 26′ N.—Ptol. IV. vii. 28]. The reading of the MS. is ἡ Τισηβαρικὴ which Müller rejects because the name nowhere occurs in any work, and because if *Barbaria* is not mentioned here, our author could not afterwards (Section 5) say ἡ ἄλλη Βαρβαρία. The *Agriophagoi* who lived in the interior are mentioned by Pliny (vi. 35), who says that they lived principally on the flesh of panthers and lions. Vincent writes as if instead of Αγριοφάγων the reading should be Ακριδοφάγων locust-eaters, who are mentioned by Agatharkh-

idês in his *De Mari Erythraeo*, Section 58. Another inland tribe is mentioned in connection with them—the *Moskhophagoi*, who may be identified with the *Rizophagoi* or *Spermato-phagoi* of the same writer, who were so named because they lived on roots of the tender suckers and buds of trees, called in Greek μόσχοι. This being a term applied also to the young of animals, Vincent was led to think that this tribe fed on the brinde or flesh cut out of the living animal as described by Bruce.

3. Below the Moskhophagoi, near the sea, lies a little trading town distant from Berenîkê about 4000 stadia, called Ptolemaïs Thêrôn, from which, in the days of the Ptolemies, the hunters employed by them used to go up into the interior to catch elephants. In this mart is procured the true (or marine) tortoise-shell, and the land kind also, which, however, is scarce, of a white colour, and smaller size. A little ivory is also sometimes obtainable, resembling that of Adouli. This place has no port, and is approachable only by boats.

(3) To the south of the Moskhophagoi lies *Ptolemaïs Thêrôn*, or, as it is called by Pliny, *Ptolemaïs Epitheras*. [On Er-rih island, lat. 18° 9′ N., long 38° 27′ E., are the ruins of an ancient town—probably Ptolemaïs Therôn—Müller however places Suche here.—Ptol. I. viii. 1.; IV. vii. 7; VIII. xvi. 10]. It was originally an Ethiopian village, but was extended and fortified by Ptolemy Philadelphos, who made it the depôt of the elephant trade, for which its situation on the skirts of the great Nubian forest, where these animals abounded, rendered it peculiarly suitable. The Egyptians before this had imported their elephants from Asia, but as the supply was precarious, and the cost of importation very great, Philadelphos made the most tempting offers to the Ethiopian elephant-hunters (Elephantophagoi) to induce them to abstain from eating the animal, or to reserve at least a portion of them for the royal stables. They rejected however all his solicitations, declaring that even for all Egypt they would not forego the luxury of their repast. The king resolved thereupon to procure his supplies by employing hunters of his own.

4. Leaving Ptolemaïs Thêrôn we are conducted, at the distance of about 3000 stadia, to Adouli, a regular and established port of trade situated on a deep bay the direction of which is due south. Facing this, at a distance seaward of about 200 stadia from the inmost recess of the bay, lies an island called Oreinê (or 'the mountainous'), which runs on either side parallel with the mainland. Ships, that come to trade with Adouli, now-a-days anchor here, to avoid being attacked from the shore; for in former times when they used to anchor at the very head of the bay, beside an island called Diodôros, which was so close to land that the sea was fordable, the neighbouring barbarians, taking advantage of this, would run across to attack the ships at their moorings. At the distance of 20 stadia from the sea, opposite Oreinê, is the village of Adouli, which is not of any great size, and inland from this a three days' journey is a city, Kolöê, the first market where ivory can

be procured. From Kolöê it takes a journey of five days to reach the metropolis of the people called the A u x u m i t a e , whereto is brought, through the province called K y ê n e i o n , all the ivory obtained on the other side of the Nile, before it is sent on to Adouli. The whole mass, I may say, of the elephants and rhinoceroses which are killed *to supply the trade* frequent the uplands *of the interior*, though at rare times they are seen near the coast, even in the neighbourhood of Adouli. Besides the islands already mentioned, a cluster consisting of many small ones lies out in the sea to the right of this port. They bear the name of A l a l a i o u , and yield the tortoises with which the I k h t h y o p h a g o i supply the market.

(4) Beyond *P t o l e m a ï s   T h ê r ô n* occurs *A d o u l ê*, at a distance, according to the *Periplûs*, of 3000 stadia—a somewhat excessive estimate. The place is called also *A d o u l e i* and more commonly Adoulis by ancient writers (Ptol. IV. vii. 8; VIII. xvi. 11). It is represented by the modern Thulla or Zula [pronounced Azule,—lat. 15° 12′-15° 15′ N., long. 39° 36′ E.].—To the West of this, according to Lord Valentia and Mr. Salt, there are to be found the remains of an ancient city. It was situated on the *A d o u l i k o s   K o l p o s* (Ptol. I. xv. 11.; IV. vii. 8), now called Annesley Bay, the best entrance into Abyssinia. It was erroneously placed by D'Anville at Dokhnau or Harkiko, close to Musawwâ [lat. 15° 35′ N.] There is much probability in the supposition that it was founded by a party of those Egyptians who, as we learn from Herodotos (II. 30), to the number of 240,000 fled from their country in the days of Psammêtikhos (B. C. 671-617) and went to as great a distance beyond Meroë, the capital of Ethiopia, as Meroë is beyond Elephantinê. This is the account which Pliny (VI. 3-4) gives of its foundation, adding that it was the greatest emporium of the *T r o g l o d y t e s* , and distant from *P t o l e m a ï s* a five days' voyage, which by the ordinary reckoning is 2,500 stadia. It was an emporium for rhinoceros' hides, ivory and tortoise-shell. It had not only a large sea-borne traffic, but was also a caravan station for the traffic of the interior of Africa. Under the Romans it was the haven of *A u x u m ê* (Ptol. IV. vii. 25,—written also Auxumis, Axumis), now Axum, the capital of the kingdom of Tigre in Abyssinia. *A u x u m ê* was the chief centre of the trade with the interior of Africa in gold-dust, ivory, leather, hides and aromatics. It was rising to great prosperity and power about the time the *Periplûs* was written, which is the earliest work extant in which it is mentioned. It was probably founded by the Egyptian exiles already referred to. Its remaining monuments are perfectly Egyptian and not pastoral, Troglodytik, Greek, or Arabian in their character. Its name at the same time retains traces of the term *A s m a k* , by which, as we learn from Herodotos, those exiles were designated, and Heeren considers it to have been one of the numerous priest-colonies which were sent out from Meroë.

At Adouli was a celebrated monument, a throne of white marble with a slab of basanite stone behind it, both covered with Greek characters, which in the sixth century of our era were copied by *Kosmas Indikopleustês*. The passage in Kosmos relating to this begins thus: "*Adulê* is a city of Ethiopia and the port of communication with *Axiômis*, and the whole nation of which that city is the capital. In this port we carry on our trade from Alexandria and the Elanitik Gulf. The town itself is about a mile from the shore, and as you enter it on the Western side which leads from *Axiômis*, there is still remaining a chair or throne which appertained to one of the Ptolemys who had subjected this country to his authority." The first portion of the inscription records that Ptolemy Euergetês (247-222 B.C.) received from the Troglodyte Arabs and Ethiopians certain elephants which his father, the second king of the Makedonian dynasty, and himself had taken in hunting in the region of ADULÊ and trained to war in their own kingdom. The second portion of the inscription commemorates the conquests of an anonymous Ethiopian king in Arabia and Ethiopia as far as the frontier of Egypt. *Adouli*, it is known for certain, received its name from a tribe so designated which formed a part of the *Danakil* shepherds who are still found in the neighbourhood of Annesley Bay, in the island of Diset [lat. 15° 28′, long. 30° 45′, the Diodôros perhaps of the *Periplûs*] opposite which is the town or station of Masawâ (anc. Saba) [lat. 15° 37′ N., long. 39° 28′ E.], and also in the archipelago of *Dhalak*, called in the *Periplûs*, the islands of *Alalaiou*. The merchants of Egypt, we learn from the work, first traded at Masawwâ but afterwards removed to Oreinê for security. This is an islet in the south of the Bay of Masawwâ, lying 20 miles from the coast; it is a rock as its name imports, and is of considerable elevation.

Aduli being the best entrance into Abyssinia, came prominently into notice during the late Abyssinian war. Beke thus speaks of it, "In our recent visit to Abyssinia I saw quite enough to confirm the opinion I have so long entertained, that when the ancient Greeks founded Adule or Adulis at the mouth of the river Hadâs, now only a river bed except during the rains, though a short way above there is rain all the year round, they knew that they possessed one of the keys of Abyssinia."

5. Below Adouli, about 800 stadia, occurs another very deep bay, at the entrance of which on the right are vast accumulations of sand, wherein is found deeply embedded the Opsian stone, which is not obtainable anywhere else. The king of all this country, from the M o s k h o p h a g o i to the other end of B a r - b a r i a, is Z ô s k a l ê s, a man at once of penurious habits and of a grasping disposition, but otherwise honourable in his dealings and instructed in the Greek language.

(5) At a distance of about 100 miles beyond *A d o u l i* the coast is indented by another bay now known as *H a n f e l a h* bay [near Râs Hanfelah in lat. 14° 44′, long. 40° 49′ E.] about 100 miles from Annesley Bay and opposite an island called Daramsas or Hanfelah. It has wells of good water and a small lake of fresh water after the rains; the coast is inhabited by the Dummoeta, a tribe of the Danakil. This is the locality where, and where only, the Opsian or Obsidian stone was to be found. Pliny calls it an unknown bay, because traders making for the ports of Arabia passed it by without deviating from their course to enter it. He was aware, as well as our author, that it contained the Opsian stone, of which he gives an account, already produced in the introduction.

6. These articles which these places import are the following:—

Ἱμάτια βαρβαρικα, ἄγναφα τὰ ἐν Αἰγύπτῳ γινόμενα—Cloth undressed, of Egyptian manufacture, for the Barbarian market.

Στολὰι Ἀρσινοητικὰι—Robes manufactured at Arsinoê.

Ἀβόλλαι νόθοι χρωμάτιναι—Cloaks, made of a poor cloth imitating a better quality, and dyed.

Λέντια—Linens.

Δικρόσσια—Striped cloths and fringed. Mantles with a double fringe.

Λιθίας ὑαλῆς πλείονα γένη καὶ ἄλλης μορρίνης, τῆς γινομένης ἐν Διοσπόλει—Many sorts of glass or crystal, and of that other transparent stone called Myrrhina, made at Diospolis.

Ὀρείχαλκος—Yellow copper, for ornaments and cut into pieces to pass for money.

Μελίεφθα χαλκᾶ—Copper fused with honey: for culinary vessels and cutting into bracelets and anklets worn by certain classes of women.

Σίδηρος—Iron. Consumed in making spearheads for hunting the elephant and other animals and in making weapons of war.

Πελύκια—Hatchets.

Σκέπαρνα—Adzes.

Μάχαιραι—Swords.

Ποτήρια χαλκᾶ στρογγύλα μεγάλα—Drinking vessels of brass, large and round.

Δηνάριον ὀλίγον—A small quantity of denarii: for the use of merchants resident in the country.

Οἶνος Λαοδικηνὸς καὶ Ἰταλικὸς οὗ πολὺς—Wine, Laodikean, *i.e.* Syrian, from Laodike, (now Latakia) and Italian, but not much.

Ἔλαιον οὐ πολύ—Oil, but not much.

Ἀργυρώματα καὶ χρυσώματα τοπικῷ ῥυθμῷ κατεσκευασμέναι—Gold and silver plate made according to the fashion of the country for the king.

Ἀβόλλαι—Cloaks for riding or for the camp.

Καυνάκαι ἁπλοῖ—Dresses simply made of skins with the hair or fur on. These two articles of dress are not of much value.

These articles are imported from the interior parts of Ariakê:—

Σίδηρος Ἰνδικὸς—Indian iron.

Στόμωμα—Sharp blades.

Ὀθόνιον Ἰνδικὸν τὸ πλατύτερον, ἡ λεγομένη μοναχὴ.—Monakhê,[17] Indian cotton cloth of great width.

Σαγματογῆναι—Cotton for stuffing.

Περιζώματα—Sashes or girdles.

Καυνάκαι—Dresses of skin with the hair or fur on.

Μολόχινα—Webs of cloth mallow-tinted.

Σινδόνες ὀλίγαι—Fine muslins in small quantity.

Λάκκος χρωμάτινος—Gum-lac: yielding Lake.

The articles locally produced for export are ivory, tortoise-shell, and rhinoceros. Most of the goods which supply the market arrive any time from January to September—that is, from Tybi to Thôth. The best season, however, for ships from Egypt to put in here is about the month of September.

7. From this bay the Arabian Gulf trends eastward, and at A u a l i t ê s is contracted to its narrowest. At a distance of about 4000 stadia (*from Adouli*), if you still sail along the same coast, you reach other marts of B a r b a r i a , called the marts beyond (*the Straits*), which occur in successive order, and which, though harbourless, afford at certain seasons of the year good and safe anchorage. The first district you come to is that called A u a l i t ê s , where the passage across the strait to the opposite point of Arabia is shortest. Here is a small port of trade, called, like the district, A u a l i t ê s , which can be approached only by little boats and rafts. The imports of this place are—

Ὑαλὴ λίθια σύμμικτος—Flint glass of various sorts.

Χυλός] Διοσπολιτικῆς ὄμφακος—Juice of the sour grape of Diospolis.

Ἱμάτια βαρβαρικὰ σύμμικτα γεγναμμένα—Cloths of different kinds worn in Barbaria dressed by the fuller.

Σῖτος—Corn.

Οἶνος—Wine.

Κασσίτερος ὀλίγος—A little tin.

The exports, which are sometimes conveyed on rafts across the straits by the B e r b e r s themselves to O k ê l i s and M o u z a on the opposite coast, are—

---

[17] Bruce, *Travels*, vol. III., p. 62.—J. B.

Ἀρώματα—Odoriferous gums.

Ἐλέφας ὀλίγος—Ivory in small quantity.

Χελώνη—Tortoise-shell.

Σμύρνα ἐλαχίστη διαφέρουσα δὲ τῆς ἄλλης—Myrrh in very small quantity, but of the finest sort.

Μάκειρ—Macer.

The barbarians forming the population of the place are *rude and* lawless men.

(6, 7) From this bay the coast of the gulf, according to our author, has a more easterly direction to the Straits, the distance to which from Adouli is stated at 4,000 stadia, an estimate much too liberal. In all this extent of coast the *Periplûs* mentions only the bay of the Opsian-stones and conducts us at once from thence to Aualités at the straits. Strabo however, and Juba, and Pliny, and Ptolemy mention several places in this tract, such as *Arsinoë, Berenîkê, Epideirês*, the Grove of Eumenês, the Chase of Puthangelos, the Territory of the Elephantophagoi, &c. The straits are called by Ptolemy *Deirê* or *Dêrê* (*i. e.* the neck), a word which from its resemblance in sound to the Latin *Dirae* has sometimes been explained to mean "the terrible." (I. xv. 11; IV. vii. 9; VIII. xvi. 12). "The *Periplûs*," Vincent remarks, "makes no mention of Deirê, but observes that the point of contraction is close to *Abalitês* or the Abalitik mart; it is from this mart that the coast of Africa falling down first to the South and curving afterwards towards the East is styled the Bay of *Aualitês* by Ptolemy, (IV. vii. 10, 20, 27, 30, 39,) but in the *Periplûs* this name is confined to a bay immediately beyond the straits which D'Anville has likewise inserted in his map, but which I did not fully understand till I obtained Captain Cook's chart and found it perfectly consistent with the *Periplûs*." It is the gulf of Tejureh or Zeyla.

The tract of country extending from the Straits to Cape Arômata (now Guardafui) is called at the present day *Adel*. It is described by Strabo (XVI. iv. 14), who copies his account of it from Artemidoros. He mentions no emporium, nor any of the names which occur in the *Periplûs* except the haven of Daphnous. [Bandar Mariyah, lat. 11° 46′ N., long. 50° 38′ E.] He supplies however many particulars regarding the region which are left unnoticed by our author as having no reference to commerce—particulars, however, which prove that these parts which were resorted to in the times of the Ptolemies for elephant-hunting were much better known to the ancients than they were till quite recently known to ourselves. Ptolemy gives nearly the same series of names (IV. vii. 9, 10) as the *Periplûs*, but with some discrepancies in the matter of their distances which he does not so accurately state. His list is: *Dêre*, a city; *Abalitês* or Aualitês, a mart; *Malaô*, a mart;

M o u n d o u or *M o n d o u* , a mart; Mondou, an island; Mosulon, a cape and a mart; *K o b ê* , a mart; *E l e p h a s* , a mountain; *A k k a n a i* or Akannai, a mart; *A r ô m a t a* , a cape and a mart.

The mart of *A b a l i t ê s* is represented by the modern *Z e y l a* [lat. 11° 22′ N., long. 43° 29′ E., 79 miles from the straits.] On the N. shore of the gulf are Abalit and Tejureh. Abalit is 43 miles from the straits, and Tejureh 27 miles from Abalit. This is the *Z o u i l e h* of Ebn Haukal and the *Z a l e g h* of Idrisi. According to the *Periplûs* it was near the straits, but Ptolemy has fixed it more correctly at the distance from them of 50 or 60 miles.

8. Beyond Aualitês there is another mart, superior to it, called M a l a ô , at a distance by sea of 800 stadia. The anchorage is an open road, sheltered, however, by a cape protruding eastward. The people are of a more peaceable disposition than their neighbours. The imports are such as have been already specified, with the addition of—

Πλείονες χιτῶνες—Tunics in great quantity.

Σάγοι Ἀρσινοητικοι γεγναμμένοι καὶ βεβαμμένοι—Coarse cloaks (or blankets) manufactured at Arsinoê, prepared by the fuller and dyed.

Μελίεφθα ὀλίγα—A few utensils made of copper fused with honey.

Σίδερος—Iron.

Δηνάριον οὐ πολὺ χρυσοῦντε καὶ ἀργυροῦν—Specie,—gold and silver, but not much.

The exports from this locality are—

Σμύρνα—Myrrh.

Λίβανος ὁ περατικος ὀλίγὸς—Frankincense *which we call peratic, i.e.* from beyond the straits, a little only.

Κασσία σκληροτέρα—Cinnamon of a hard grain.

Δούακα—Douaka (*an inferior kind of cinnamon*).

Κάγκαμον—The gum (*for fumigation*) *kangkamon.* 'Dekamalli,' gum.

Μάκειρ—The spice *macer,* which is carried to Arabia.

Σώματα σπανίως—Slaves, a few.

(8) *M a l a ô* as a mart was much superior to Abalitês, from which our author estimates its distance to be 800 stadia, though it is in reality greater. From the description he gives of its situation it must be identified with Berbereh [lat. 10° 25′ N., long. 45° 1′ E.] now the most considerable mart on this part of the coast. Vincent erroneously places it between Zeyla and the straits.

9. Distant from M a l a ô two days′ sail is the trading port of M o u n d o u , where ships find a safer anchorage by mooring at an island which lies very close to shore. The exports and imports are similar to those of the preceding marts, with

the addition of the fragrant gum called *Mokrotou*, a peculiar product of the place. The native traders here are uncivilized in their manners.

(9) The next mart after Malaô is *M o u n d o u*, which, as we learn from Ptolemy, was also the name of an adjacent island—that which is now called Meyet or Burnt-island [lat. 11° 12′ N., long. 47° 17′ E., 10 miles east of Bandar Jedid].

10. After *M o u n d o u*, if you sail eastward as before for two or three days, there comes next *M o s u l l o n*, where it is difficult to anchor. It imports the same sorts of commodities as have been already mentioned, and also utensils of silver and others of iron but not so many, and glass-ware. It exports a vast amount of cinnamon (whence it is a port requiring ships of heavy burden) and other fragrant and aromatic products, besides tortoise-shell, but in no great quantity, and the incense called *mokrotou* inferior to that of Moundou, and frankincense brought from parts further distant, and ivory and myrrh though in small quantity.

(10) At a distance beyond it of two or three days′ sail occurs *M o s u l o n*, which is the name both of a mart and of a promontory. It is mentioned by Pliny (VI. 34), who says: "Further on is the bay of *A b a l i t ê s*, the island of *D i o d ô r u s* and other islands which are desert. On the mainland, which has also deserts, occur a town *G a z a* [Bandar Gazim, long. 49° 13′ E.], the promontory and port of *M o s y l o n*, whence cinnamon is exported. Sesostris led his army to this point and no further. Some writers place one town of Ethiopia beyond it, Baricaza, which lies on the coast. According to Juba the Atlantic Sea begins at the promontory of Mossylon." Juba evidently confounded this promontory with Cape Arômata, and Ptolemy, perhaps in consequence, makes its projection more considerable than it is. D′Anville and Gosselin thought *M o s s u l o n* was situated near the promontory Mete, where is a river, called the Soal, which they supposed preserved traces of the name of Mossulon. This position however cannot be reconciled with the distances given in the *Periplûs*, which would lead us to look for it where Guesele is placed in the latest description given of this coast. Vincent on very inadequate grounds would identify it with Barbara or Berbera. [Müller places it at Bandar Barthe and Ras Antarah, long. 49° 35′ E.]

11. After leaving *M o s u l l o n*, and sailing past a place called *N e i l o p t o l-e m a i o s*, and past *T a p a t ê g ê* and the Little Laurel-grove, you are conducted in two days to Capo *E l e p h a n t*. Here is a stream called *E l e p h a n t* River, and the Great Laurel-grove called *A k a n n a i*, where, and where only, is produced the *peratic* frankincense. The supply is most abundant, and it is of the very finest quality.

(11) After Mosulon occurs Cape Elephant, at some distance beyond *N e i l o p t o l e m a i o s, T a p a t ê g ê*, and the Little Laurel-grove. At the Cape is a river and the Great Laurel-grove called

A k a n n a i. Strabo in his account of this coast mentions a Neilo-spotamia which however can hardly be referred to this particular locality which pertains to the region through which the Khori or San Pedro flows, of which Idrisi (I. 45) thus writes: "At two journeys' distance from Markah in the desert is a river which is subject to risings like the Nile and on the banks of which they sow dhorra." Regarding Cape Elephant Vincent says, "it is formed by a mountain conspicuous in the Portuguese charts under the name of Mount Felix or Felles from the native term Jibel Fîl, literally, Mount Elephant. The cape [Ras Filik, 800 ft. high, lat. 11° 57′ N., long. 50° 37′ E.] is formed by the land jutting up to the North from the direction of the coast which is nearly East and West, and from its northernmost point the land falls off again South-East to Râs 'Asir — Cape Guardafui, the Arômata of the ancients. We learn from Captain Saris, an English navigator, that there is a river at Jibel Fîl. In the year 1611 he stood into a bay or harbour there which he represents as having a safe entrance for three ships abreast: he adds also that several sorts of gums very sweet in burning were still purchased by the Indian ships from Cambay which touched here for that purpose in their passage to Mocha." The passage in the *Periplûs* where these places are mentioned is very corrupt. Vincent, who regards the greater *D a p h n ô n* (Laurel-grove) as a river called *A k a n n a i*, says, "Neither place or distance is assigned to any of these names, but we may well allot the rivers Daphnôn and Elephant to the synonymous town and cape; and these may be represented by the modern Mete and Santa Pedro." [Müller places Elephas at Ras el Fîl, long. 50° 37′ E., and Akannai at Ulûlah Bandar, long. 50° 56′ E., but they may be represented by Ras Ahileh, where a river enters through a lagoon in 11° 46′, and Bonah, a town with wells of good water in lat. 11° 58′ N., long. 50° 51′ E.]

12. After this, the coast now inclining to the south, succeeds the mart of A r ô m a t a , and a bluff headland running out eastward which forms the termination of the Barbarine coast. The roadstead is an open one, and at certain seasons dangerous, as the place lies exposed to the north wind. A coming storm gives warning of its approach by a peculiar prognostic, for the sea turns turbid at the bottom and changes its colour. When this occurs, all hasten for refuge to the great promontory called T a b a i , which affords a secure shelter. The imports into this mart are such as have been already mentioned; while its products are cinnamon, gizeir (*a finer sort of cinnamon*), asuphê (*an ordinary sort*), fragrant gums, magla, motô (*an inferior cinnamon*), and frankincense.

(12) We come now to the great projection Cape Arômata, which is a continuation of Mount Elephant. It is called in Arabic *J e r d H a f û n* or Ras Asir; in Idrisi, *C a r f o u n a*, whence the name by which it is generally known. [The South point 11° 40′

is Râs Shenarif or Jerd Hafûn; the N. point 11° 51′ is Râs 'Asir.]
It formed the limit of the knowledge of this coast in the time of
Strabo, by whom it is called *Notou Keras* or South Horn. It is
described as a very high bluff point and as perpendicular as if it
were scarped. [Jerd Hafûn is 2500 feet high.] The current comes
round it out of the gulf with such violence that it is not to be
stemmed without a brisk wind, and during the South-West Monsoon, the moment you are past the Cape to the North there is a
stark calm with insufferable heat. The current below Jerd Hafûn is
noticed by the *Periplûs* as setting to the South, and is there perhaps
equally subject to the change of the monsoon. With this account of
the coast from the straits to the great Cape may be compared that
which has been given by Strabo, XVI. iv. 14:

"From *Deirê* the next country is that which bears aromatic
plants. The first produces myrrh and belongs to the *Ichthyoph-
agi* and *Creophagi*. It bears also the persea, peach or Egyptian almond, and the Egyptian fig. Beyond is *Licha*, a hunting
ground for elephants. There are also in many places standing
pools of rainwater. When these are dried up, the elephants with
their trunks and tusks dig holes and find water. On this coast
there are two very large lakes extending as far as the promontory
Pytholaus. One of them contains salt water and is called a sea; the
other fresh water and is the haunt of hippopotami and crocodiles.
On the margin grows the papyrus. The ibis is seen in the neighbourhood of this place. Next is the country which produces frankincense; it has a promontory and a temple with a grove of poplars.
In the inland parts is a tract along the banks of a river bearing the
name of *Isis*, and another that of *Nilus*, both of which produce
myrrh and frankincense. Also a lagoon filled with water from the
mountains. Next the watch-post of the Lion and the port of *Py-
thangelus*. The next tract bears the false cassia. There are many
tracts in succession on the sides of rivers on which frankincense
grows, and rivers extending to the cinnamon country. The river
which bounds this tract produces rushes (φλους) in great abundance. Then follows another river and the port of *Daphnus*,
and a valley called *Apollo*'s which bears besides frankincense,
myrrh and cinnamon. The latter is more abundant in places far
in the interior. Next is the mountain *Elephas*, a mountain projecting into the sea and a creek; then follows the large harbour of
Psygmus, a watering place called that of *Kunocephali* and
the last promontory of this coast *Notu-ceras* (or the Southern
Horn). After doubling this cape towards the south we have no
more descriptions of harbours or places because nothing is known
of the sea-coast beyond this point." [Bohn's *Transl.*] According to
Gosselin, the Southern Horn corresponds with the Southern Cape
of Bandel-caus, where commences the desert coast of Ajan, the

ancient *Azania*.

According to the *Periplûs* Cape *Arômata* marked the termination of *Barbaria* and the beginning of *Azania*. Ptolemy however distinguishes them differently, defining the former as the interior and the latter as the sea-board of the region to which these names were applied.

The description of the Eastern Coast of Africa which now follows is carried, as has been already noticed, as far as *Rhapta*, a place about 6 degrees South of the Equator, but which Vincent places much farther South, identifying it with Kilwa.

The places named on this line of coast are: a promontory called *Tabai*, a Khersonesos; *Opônê*, a mart; the Little and the Great *Apokopa*; the Little and the Great Coast; the *Dromoi* or courses of *Azania* (first that of *Serapiôn*, then that of *Nikôn*); a number of rivers; a succession of anchorages, seven in number; the *Paralaoi* islands; a strait or canal; the island of *Menouthias*; and then *Rhapta*, beyond which, as the author conceived, the ocean curved round Africa until it met and amalgamated with the Hesperian or Western Ocean.

13. If, on sailing from *Tabai*, you follow the coast of the peninsula *formed by the promontory*, you are carried by the force of a strong current to another mart 400 stadia distant, called *Opônê*, which imports the commodities already mentioned, but produces most abundantly cinnamon, spice, *motô*, slaves of a very superior sort, chiefly for the Egyptian market, and tortoise-shell of small size but in large quantity and of the finest quality known.

(13) Tabai, to which the inhabitants of the Great Cape fled for refuge on the approach of a storm, cannot, as Vincent and others have supposed, be Cape Orfui, for it lay at too great a distance for the purpose. The projection is meant which the Arabs call Banna. [Or, Tabai may be identified with Râs Shenarif, lat. 11° 40′ N.] Tabai, Müller suggests, may be a corruption for Tabannai.

"From the foreign term Banna," he says, "certain Greeks in the manner of their countrymen invented *Panos* or *Panôn* or Panô or Panôna Kômê. Thus in Ptolemy (I. 17 and IV. 7) after Arômata follows *Panôn Kômê*, which Mannert has identified with Benna. [Khor Banneh is a salt lake, with a village, inside Râs Ali Beshgêl, lat. 11° 9′ N., long. 51° 9′ E.] Stephen of Byzantium may be compared, who speaks of *Panos* as a village on the Red Sea which is also called *Panôn*." The conjecture, therefore, of Letronnius that *Panôn Kômê* derived its name from the large apes found there, called *Pânes*, falls to the ground. *Opônê* was situated on the Southern shores of what the *Periplûs* calls a Khersonese, which can only be the projection now called *Ras Hafûn* or Cape D'Orfui (lat. 10° 25′ N.). Ptolemy (I. 17) gives the distance of *O p ô n ê* from *P a n ô n   K ô m ê* at a 6 days' journey, from which according to the *Periplûs* it was only 400 stadia distant. That the text of Ptolemy is here corrupt cannot be doubted, for in his tables the distance between the two places is not far from that which is given in the *Periplûs*. Probably, as Müller conjectures, he wrote ὁδόν ἡμέρας (a day's journey) which was converted into ὁδόν ἡμερ. ς′ (a six-days' journey).

14. Ships set sail from Egypt for all these ports beyond the straits about the month of July—that is, Epiphi. The same markets are also regularly supplied with the products of places far beyond them—A r i a k ê and B a r u g a z a . These products are—

Σῖτος—Corn.

Ὄρυζα[18]—Rice.

Βούτυρον—Butter, i. e. *ghî*.

Ἔλαιον σησάμινον—Oil of sesamum.

Ὀθόνιον ἥ τε μοναχὴ καὶ ἡ σαγματογήνη—Fine cotton called *Monakhê*, and a coarse kind for stuffing called *Sagmatogene*.

Περιζώματα—Sashes or girdles.

Μέλι τὸ καλάμινον τὸ λεγόμενον σάκχαρι—The honey of a reed, called *sugar*.

Some traders undertake voyages for this commerce expressly, while others, as they sail along the coast *we are describing*, exchange their cargoes for such others as they can procure. There is no king who reigns paramount over all this region, but each separate seat of trade is ruled by an independent despot of its own.

> (14) At this harbour is introduced the mention of the voyage which was annually made between the coast of India and Africa in days previous to the appearance of the Greeks on the Indian Ocean, which has already been referred to.

15. After O p ô n ê , the coast now trending more to the south, you come first to what are called the little and the great A p o k o p a (or Bluffs) of A z a n i a , where there are no harbours, but only roads in which ships can conveniently anchor. The navigation of this coast, the direction of which is now to the south-west, occupies six days. Then follow the Little Coast and the Great Coast, occupying other six days, when in due order succeed the D r o m o i (or Courses) of A z a n i a , the one going by the name of S a r a p i ô n , and the other by that of N i k ô n . Proceeding thence, you pass the mouths of numerous rivers, and a succession of other roadsteads lying apart one from another a day's distance either by sea or by land. There are seven of them altogether, and they reach on to the P u r a l a o i islands and the *narrow strait* called the Canal, beyond which, where the coast changes its direction from south-west slightly more to south, you are conducted by a voyage of two days and two nights to M e n o u t h i a s , an island stretching towards sunset, and

---

[18] From the Tamil *ariśi*, rice deprived of the husk.—*Caldwell*.

distant from the mainland about 300 stadia. It is low-lying and woody, has rivers, and a vast variety of birds, and yields the mountain tortoise, but it has no wild beasts at all, except only crocodiles, which, however, are quite harmless. The boats are here made of planks sewn together attached to a keel formed of a single log of wood, and these are used for fishing and for catching turtle. This is also caught in another mode, peculiar to the island, by lowering wicker-baskets instead of nets, and fixing them against the mouths of the cavernous rocks which lie out in the sea confronting the beach.

(15) After leaving *O p ô n ê* the coast first runs due south, then bends to the south-west, and here begins the coast which is called the Little and the Great *A p o k o p a* or Bluffs of *A z a n i a*, the voyage along which occupies six days. This rocky coast, as we learn from recent explorations, begins at *R â s   M a b b e r* [about lat. 9° 25′ N.], which is between 70 and 80 miles distant from Ras Hafûn and extends only to *R â s - u l - K h e i l* [about lat. 7° 45′ N.], which is distant from Râs Mabber about 140 miles or a voyage of three or four days only. The length of this rocky coast (called *H a z - i n e* by the Arabs) is therefore much exaggerated in the *Periplûs*. From this error we may infer that our author, who was a very careful observer, had not personally visited this coast. Ptolemy, in opposition to Marînos as well as the *Periplûs*, recognizes but one *A p o k o p a*, which he speaks of as a bay. Müller concludes an elaborate note regarding the *A p o k o p a* by the following quotation from the work of Owen, who made the exploration already referred to, "It is strange that the descriptive term *H a z i n e* should have produced the names *A j a n*, *A z a n* and *A z a n i a* in many maps and charts, as the country never had any other appellation than *B a r r a   S o m â l i* or the land of the *S o m â l i*, a people who have never yet been collected under one government, and whose limits of subjection are only within bow-shot of individual chiefs. The coast of Africa from the Red Sea to the river Juba is inhabited by the tribe called *S o m â l i*. They are a mild people of pastoral habits and confined entirely to the coast; the whole of the interior being occupied by an untameable tribe of savages called *G a l l a*."

The coast which follows the *A p o k o p a*, called the Little and the Great *A i g i a l o s* or Coast, is so desolate that, as Vincent remarks, not a name occurs on it, neither is there an anchorage noticed, nor the least trace of commerce to be found. Yet it is of great extent—a six days' voyage according to the *Periplûs*, but, according to Ptolemy, who is here more correct, a voyage of eight days, for, as we have seen, the *Periplûs* has unduly extended the *A p o k o p a* to the South.

Next follow the *D r o m o i* or Courses of *A z a n i a*, the first called that of *S e r a p i ô n* and the other that of *N i k ô n*. Ptolemy interposes a bay between the Great Coast and the port of *S e r a -*

p i ô n, on which he states there was an emporium called *E s s i - n a* — a day's sail distant from that port. Essina, it would therefore appear, must have been somewhere near where *M a k d a s h û* [Magadoxo, lat. 2° 3′ N.] was built by the Arabs somewhere in the eighth century A.D. The station called that of *N i k ô n* in the *Periplûs* appears in Ptolemy as the mart of *T o n i k ê*. These names are not, as some have supposed, of Greek origin, but distortions of the native appellations of the places into names familiar to Greek ears. That the Greeks had founded any settlements here is altogether improbable. At the time when the *Periplûs* was written all the trade of these parts was in the hands of the Arabs of *M o u z a*. The port of *S e r a p i ô n* may be placed at a promontory which occurs in 1° 40′ of N. lat. From this, *T o n i k ê*, according to the tables of Ptolemy, was distant 45′, and its position must therefore have agreed with that of *T o r r e* or Torra of our modern maps.

Next occurs a succession of rivers and roadsteads, seven in number, which being passed we are conducted to the *P u r a l a ä n* Islands, and what is called a canal or channel (διώρυξ). These islands are not mentioned elsewhere. They can readily be identified with the two called *M a n d a* and *L a m o u*, which are situate at the mouths of large rivers, and are separated from the mainland and from each other by a narrow channel. Vincent would assign a Greek origin to the name of these islands. "With a very slight alteration," he says, "of the reading, the Puralian Islands (Πῦρ ἅλιον, *marine fire*,) are the islands of the Fiery Ocean, and nothing seems more consonant to reason than for a Greek to apply the name of the Fiery Ocean to a spot which was the centre of the Torrid Zone and subject to the perpendicular rays of an equinoctial sun." [The Juba islands run along the coast from Juba to about Lat. 1° 50′ S., and Manda bay and island is in Lat. 2° 12′ S.]

Beyond these islands occurs, after a voyage of two days and two nights, the island of *M e n o u t h i a s* or *M e n o u t h e s i a s*, which it has been found difficult to identify with any certainty. "It is," says Vincent, "the *Eitenediommenouthesias* of the *Periplûs*, a term egregiously strange and corrupted, but out of which the commentators unanimously collect Menoothias, whatever may be the fate of the remaining syllables. That this Menoothias," he continues, "must have been one of the Zangibar islands is indubitable; for the distance from the coast of all three, Pemba, Zangibar, and Momfia, affords a character which is indelible; a character applicable to no other island from Guardafui to Madagascar." He then identifies it with the island of Zangibar, lat. 6° 5′ S., in preference to Pemba, 5° 6′ S., which lay too far out of the course, and in preference to Momfia, 7° 50′ S. (though more doubtfully), because of its being by no means conspicuous, whereas Zangibar was so prominent and obvious above the other two, that it might well attract the particular attention of navigators, and its distance from the mainland is at the same time so nearly in accordance with that given in the *Periplûs* as to counterbalance all other objections. A writer in Smith's *Classical Geography*, who seems to have overlooked the indications of the distances both of Ptolemy and the *Periplûs*, assigns it a position much further to the north than is reconcilable with these distances. He places it about a degree south from the mouth of the River Juba or Govind, just where an opening in the coral-reefs is now found. "The coasting voyage," he says, "steering S. W., reached the island on the east side—a proof that it was close to the main.... It is true the navigator says it was 300 stadia from the mainland; but as there is no reason to suppose that he surveyed the island, this distance must be taken to signify the estimated width of the northern inlet separating the island from the main, and this estimate is probably much exaggerated. The mode of fishing with baskets is still practised in the Juba islands and along this coast. The formation of the coast of E. Africa in these latitudes—where the hills or downs upon the coast are all formed of a coral conglomerate comprising fragments of madrepore, shell and sand, renders it likely that the island which was close to the main 16 or 17 centuries ago, should now be united to it. Granting this theory of gradual transformation of the coast-line, the M e n o u t h i a s of the *Periplûs* may be supposed to have stood in what is now the rich garden-land of S h a m b a , where the rivers carrying down mud to mingle with the marine deposit of coral drift covered the choked-up estuary with a rich soil."

The island is said in the *Periplûs* to extend towards the West, but this does not hold good either in the case of Zangibar or any other island in this part of the coast. Indeed there is no one of them in which at the present day all the characteristics of M e n o u t h i - a s are found combined. M o m f i a , for instance, which resembles it somewhat in name, and which, as modern travellers tell us, is almost entirely occupied with birds and covered with their dung, does not possess any streams of water. These are found in Zangibar. The author may perhaps have confusedly blended together the accounts he had received from his Arab informants.

16. At the distance of a two days' sail from this island lies the last of the marts of A z a n i a , called R h a p t a , a name which it derives from the sewn boats just mentioned. Ivory is procured here in the greatest abundance, and also turtle. The indigenous inhabitants are men of huge stature, who live *apart from each other*, every man ruling like a lord his own domain. The whole territory is governed by the despot of M o p h a r i t i s , because the sovereignty over it, by some right of old standing, is vested in the kingdom of what is called the First Arabia. The merchants of M o u z a farm its revenues from the king, and employ in trading

with it a great many ships of heavy burden, on board of which they have Arabian commanders and factors who are intimately acquainted with the natives and have contracted marriage with them, and know their language and the navigation of the coast.

(16) We arrive next and finally at *R h a p t a*, the last emporium on the coast known to the author. Ptolemy mentions not only a city of this name, but also a river and a promontory. The name is Greek (from ῥάπτειν, *to sew*), and was applied to the place because the vessels there in use were raised from bottoms consisting of single trunks of trees by the addition of planks which were sewn together with the fibres of the cocoa. "It is a singular fact," as Vincent remarks, "that this peculiarity should be one of the first objects which attracted the attention of the Portuguese upon their reaching this coast. They saw them first at Mozambique, where they were called *Almeidas*, but the principal notice of them in most of their writers is generally stated at Kilwa, the very spot which we have supposed to receive its name from vessels of the same construction." Vincent has been led from this coincidence to identify Rhapta with Kilwa [lat. 8° 50′ S.]. Müller however would place it not so far south, but somewhere in the Bay of Zangibar. The promontory of *R h a p t u m*, he judges from the indications of the *Periplûs* to be the projection which closes the bay in which lies the island of Zangibar, and which is now known as *M o i n a n o k a l û* or Point Pouna, lat. 7° S. The parts beyond this were unknown, and the southern coast of Africa, it was accordingly thought by the ancient geographers, began here. Another cape however is mentioned by Ptolemy remoter than Rhaptum and called *P r a - s u m* (that is the Green Cape) which may perhaps be Cape Delgado, which is noted for its luxuriant vegetation. The same author calls the people of *R h a p t a*, the *R h a p s i o i   A i t h i o p e s*. They are described in the *Periplûs* as men of lofty stature, and this is still a characteristic of the Africans of this coast. The *R h a p s i i* were, in the days of our author, subject to the people of *M o u z a* in Arabia just as their descendants are at the present day subject to the Sultan of Maskat. Their commerce moreover still maintains its ancient characteristics. It is the African who still builds and mans the ships while the Arab is the navigator and supercargo. The ivory is still of inferior quality, and the turtle is still captured at certain parts of the coast.

17. The articles imported into these marts are principally javelins manufactured at Mouza, hatchets, knives, awls, and crown glass of various sorts, to which must be added corn and wine in no small quantity landed at particular ports, not for sale, but to entertain and thereby conciliate the barbarians. The articles which these places export are ivory, in great abundance but of inferior quality to that obtained at Adouli, rhinoceros, and tortoise-shell of fine quality, second only to the

Indian, and a little *nauplius*.

18. These marts, we may say, are about the last on the coast of A z a n i a — the coast, that is, which is on your right as you sail *south* from B e r e n î k ê. For beyond these parts an ocean, hitherto unexplored, curves round towards sunset, and, stretching along the southern extremities of Ethiopia, Libya, and Africa, amalgamates with the Western Sea.

19. To the left, again, of B e r e n i k ê, if you sail eastward from M y o s - H o r m o s across the adjacent gulf for two days, or perhaps three, you arrive at a place having a port and a fortress which is called L e u k ê K ô m ê, and forming the point of communication with Petra, the residence of M a l i k h a s, the king of the Nabatæans. It ranks as an emporium of trade, since small vessels come to it laden with merchandize from Arabia; and hence an officer is deputed to collect the duties which are levied on imports at the rate of twenty-five per cent. of their value, and also a centurion who commands the garrison by which the place is protected.

(18, 19) Our author having thus described the African coast as far southward as it was known on its Eastern side, reverts to *Berenikê* and enters at once on a narrative of the second voyage—that which was made thence across the Northern head of the gulf and along the coast of Arabia to the emporium of *M o u - z a* near the Straits. The course is first northward, and the parts about *B e r e n i k ê* as you bear away lie therefore now on your left hand. Having touched at *M y o s H o r m o s* the course on leaving it is shaped eastward across the gulf by the promontory *P h a r a n*, and *L e u k ê K ô m ê*[19] is reached after three or four days' sailing. This was a port in the kingdom of the Nabathæans (the Nebaioth of Scripture), situated perhaps near the mouth of the Elanitic Gulf or eastern arm of the Red Sea, now called the Gulf of Akabah. Much difference of opinion has prevailed as to its exact position, since the encroachment of the land upon the sea has much altered the line of coast here. Mannert identified it with the modern *Y e n b o* [lat. 24° 5′ N., long. 38° 3′ E., the port of Medina], Gosselin with *M o w i l a h* [lat. 27° 38′ N., long. 35° 28′ E.,] Vincent with *E y n o u n a h* [lat. 28° 3′ N., long. 35° 13′ E.—the *O n n e* of Ptolemy], Reichhard with *I s t a b e l A n t a i*, and Rüppel with *W e j h* [lat. 26° 13′ N., long. 36° 27′ E]. Müller prefers the opinion held by Bochart, D'Anville, Quatremêre, Noel des Vergers, and Ritter, who agree in placing it at the port called *H a u a r a* [lat. 24° 59′ N., long. 37° 16′ E.] mentioned by Idrisi (I. p. 332), who describes it as a village inhabited by merchants carrying on a considerable trade in earthen vases manufactured at a clay-pit in their neighbourhood. Near it lies the island of *H a s s a n i* [lat. 24° 59′ N., long. 37° 3′ E.], which, as Wellsted reports, is conspicuous from its *white* appearance. *L e u k ê K ô m ê* is mentioned by various ancient authors, as for instance Strabo, who, in a passage wherein he

---

[19] Meaning *white village*.

recounts the misfortunes which befel the expedition which Aelius led into Nabathaea, speaks of the place as a large mart to which and from which the camel traders travel with ease and in safety from *P e t r a* and back to *P e t r a* with so large a body of men and camels as to differ in no respect from an army.

The merchandize thus conveyed from *L e u k ê   K ô m ê* to *P e - t r a* was passed on to *R h i n o k o l o u r a* in Palestine near Egypt, and thence to other nations, but in his own time the greater part was transported by the Nile to *A l e x a n d r i a*. It was brought down from India and Arabia to *M y o s   H o r m o s*, whence it was first conveyed on camels to *K o p t o s* and thence by the Nile to *A l - e x a n d r i a*. The Nabathaean king, at the time when our author visited *L e u k ê   K ô m ê*, was, as he tells us, *M a l i k h a s*, a name which means 'king.' Two Petraean sovereigns so called are mentioned by Josêphos, of whom the latter was contemporary with Herod. The Malikhas of the *Periplûs* is however not mentioned in any other work. The Nabathaean kingdom was subverted in the time of Trajan, A.D. 105, us we learn from Dio Cassius (cap. lxviii. 14), and from Eutropius (viii. 2, 9), and from Ammianus Marcellinus (xiv. 8).

20. Beyond this mart, and quite contiguous to it, is the realm of Arabia, which stretches to a great distance along the coast of the Red Sea. It is inhabited by various tribes, some speaking the same language with a certain degree of uniformity, and others a language totally different. Here also, *as on the opposite continent*, the sea-board is occupied by I k h t h y o p h a g o i, who live in dispersed huts; while the men of the interior live either in villages, or where pasture can be found, and are an evil race of men, speaking two different languages. If a vessel is driven from her course upon this shore she is plundered, and if wrecked the crew on escaping to land are reduced to slavery. For this reason they are treated as enemies and captured by the chiefs and kings of Arabia. They are called K a n r a î t a i. Altogether, therefore, the navigation of this part of the Arabian coast is very dangerous: for, *apart from the barbarity of its people*, it has neither harbours nor good roadsteads, and it is foul with breakers, and girdled with rocks which render it inaccessible. For this reason when sailing south we stand off from a shore in every way so dreadful, and keep our course down the middle of the gulf, straining our utmost to reach *the more civilized part* of Arabia, which begins at Burnt Island. From this onward the people are under a regular government, and, as their country is pastoral, they keep herds of cattle and camels.

(20) At no great distance from *L e u k ê   K ô m ê* the Nabathaean realm terminates and Arabia begins. The coast is here described as most dismal, and as in every way dangerous to navigation. The inhabitants at the same time are barbarians, destitute of all humanity, who scruple not to attack and plunder wrecked ships and to make slaves of their crews if they escaped to land. The mariner therefore, shunned these inhospitable shores, and standing well

out to sea, sailed down the middle of the gulf. The tribe here spoken of was that perhaps which is represented by the *H u t e m i* of the present day, and the coast belonged to the part of Arabia now called *H e j i d* .

A more civilized region begins at an island called Burnt island, which answers to the modern Zebâyir [about lat. 15° 5′ N., long. 42° 12′ E.], an island which was till recently volcanic.

21. Beyond this tract, and on the shore of a bay which occurs at the termination of the left (or east) side of the gulf, is M o u z a , an established and notable mart of trade, at a distance south from Berenikê of not more than 12,000 stadia. The whole place is full of Arabian shipmasters and common sailors, and is absorbed in the pursuits of commerce, for with ships of its own fitting out, it trades with the marts beyond the Straits on the opposite coast, and also with B a r u g a z a .

(21) Beyond this is the great emporium called *M o u z a* , [lat. 13° 43′ N., long. 43° 5′ 14″ E.] situated in a bay near the termination of the Gulf, and at a distance from *B e r e n i k ê* of 12,000 stadia. Here the population consists almost entirely of merchants and mariners, and the place is in the highest degree commercial. The commodities of the country are rich and numerous (though this is denied by Pliny), and there is a great traffic in Indian articles brought from *B a r u g a z a* (Bharoch). This port, once the most celebrated and most frequented in Yemen, is now the village Musa about twenty-five miles north from Mokhâ, which has replaced it as a port, the foundation of which dates back no more than 400 years ago. "Twenty miles inland from Mokhâ," says Vincent, "Niebuhr discovered a Musa still existing, which he with great probability supposes to be the ancient mart now carried inland to this distance by the recession of the coast." [He must have confounded it with *J e b e l   M u s a* , due east of Mokhâ, at the commencement of the mountain country.] It is a mere village badly built. Its water is good, and is said to be drunk by the wealthier inhabitants of Mokhâ. Bochart identified *M o u z a* with the *M e - s h a* mentioned by Moses.

22. Above this a three days' journey off lies the city of S a u ê , in the district called M o p h a r i t i s . It is the residence of K h o l a i b o s , the despot of that country.

(22) The *Periplûs* notices two cities that lay inland from *M o u - z a* —the 1st *S a u ê* , the *S a v ê* of Pliny (VI. xxvi., 104), and also of Ptolemy (VI. vii., p. 411), who places it at a distance of 500 stadia S. E. of Mouza. The position and distance direct us to the city of *T a - a e s* , which lies near a mountain called Saber. *S a u ê* belonged to a district called *M a p h a r i t i s* or *M o p h a r e i t ê s* , a name which appears to survive in the modern *M h a r r a s* , which designates a mountain lying N. E. from *T a a e s* . It was ruled by *K h o l a i b o s*

(Arabicé—Khaleb), whom our author calls a tyrant, and who was therefore probably a Sheikh who had revolted from his lawful chief, and established himself as an independent ruler.

23. A journey of nine days more conducts us to S a p h a r , the metropolis of K h a r i b a ê l , the rightful sovereign of two contiguous tribes, the H o m e r i t e s and the S a b a ï t a i , and, by means of frequent embassies and presents, the friend of the Emperors.

> (23) The other city was *Saphar*, the metropolis of the *Homerîtai, i.e.* the *Himaryi*—the Arabs of Yemen, whose power was widely extended, not only in Yemen but in distant countries both to the East and West. Saphar is called *Sapphar* by Ptolemy (VI. vii.), who places it in 14° N. lat. Philostorgios calls it *Tapharon*, and Stephen of Byzantium *Tarphara*. It is now *Dhafar* or Dsoffar or Zaphar. In Edrisi (I. p. 148) it appears as *Dhofar*, and he thus writes of it:—"It is the capital of the district Jahsseb. It was formerly one of the greatest and most famous of cities. The kings of Yemen made it their residence, and there was to be seen the palace of Zeidan. These structures are now in ruins, and the population has been much decreased, nevertheless the inhabitants have preserved some remnants of their ancient riches." The ruins of the city and palace still exist in the neighbourhood of *Jerim*, which Niebuhr places in 14° 30′ N. lat. The distance from *Sauê* to *Saphar* in the *Periplûs* is a nine days' journey. Niebuhr accomplished it however in six. Perhaps, as Müller suggests, the nine days' journey is from *Mouza* to *Saphar*. The sovereign of Saphar is called by our author *Kharibaêl*, a name which is not found among the Himyaritic kings known from other sources. In Ptolemy the region is called *Elisarôn*, from a king bearing that name.

24. The mart of M o u z a has no harbour, but its sea is smooth, and the anchorage good, owing to the sandy nature of the bottom. The commodities which it imports are—

Πορφύρα, διάφορος καὶ χυδαία—Purple cloth, fine and ordinary.

Ἱματισμὶς Ἀραβικὸς χειριδωτὸς, ὅτε ἁπλοῦς καὶ ὁ κοινὸς καὶ σκοτουλάτος καὶ διάχρυσος—Garments made up in the Arabian fashion, some plain and common, and others wrought in needlework and inwoven with gold.

Κρόκος—Saffron.

Κύπερος—The aromatic rush Kyperos. (Turmeric?)

Ὀθόνιον—Muslins.

Ἀβόλλαι—Cloaks.

Λώδικες οὐ πολλαί, ἁπλοῖ τε καὶ ἐντόπιοι—Quilts, in small quantity, some plain, others adapted to the fashion of the country.

Ζῶναι σκιωταὶ—Sashes of various shades of colour.

Μύρον μέτριον—Perfumes, a moderate quantity.

Χρῆμα ἱκανὸν—Specie as much as is required.

Οἶνος—Wine.

Σῖτος οὐ πολύς—Corn, but not much.

The country produces a little wheat and a great abundance of wine. Both the king and the despot above mentioned receive presents consisting of horses, pack-saddle mules, gold plate, silver plate embossed, robes of great value, and utensils of brass. M o u z a exports its own local products—myrrh of the finest quality that has oozed in drops from the trees, both the Gabiræan and Minœan kinds; white marble (or alabaster), in addition to commodities brought from the other side of the Gulf, all such as were enumerated at A d o u l i . The most favourable season for making a voyage to Mouza is the month of September,—that is Thôth,—but there is nothing to prevent it being made earlier.

> (24) Adjacent to the Homeritai, and subject to them when the *Periplûs* was written, were the Sabæans, so famous in antiquity for their wealth, luxury and magnificence. Their country, the *S h e b a* of Scripture, was noted as the land of frankincense. Their power at one time extended far and wide, but in the days of our author they were subject to the Homerites ruled over by Kharibaêl, who was assiduous in courting the friendship of Rome.

25. If on proceeding from M o u z a you sail by the coast for about a distance of 300 stadia, there occurs, where the Arabian mainland and the opposite coast of B a r b a r i a at A u a l i t ê s now approach each other, a channel of no great length which contracts the sea and encloses it within narrow bounds. This is 60 stadia wide, and in crossing it you come midway upon the island of D i o d ô r o s , to which it is owing that the passage of the straits is in its neighbourhood exposed to violent winds which blow down from the adjacent mountains. There is situate upon the shore of the straits an Arabian village subject to the same ruler (as Mouza), O k ê l i s by name, which is not so much a mart of commerce as a place for anchorage and supplying water, and where those who are bound for the interior first land and halt to refresh themselves.

> (25) At a distance of 300 stadia beyond *M o u z a* we reach the straits where the shores of Arabia and Africa advance so near to each other that the passage between them has only, according to the *Periplûs*, a width of 60 stadia, or 7½ miles. In the midst of the passage lies the island of *D i o d ô r o s* (now Perim), which is about 4½ miles long by 2 broad, and rises 230 feet above the level of the sea. The straits, according to Moresby, are 14½ geographical miles wide at the entrance between Bab-el-Mandab Cape (near which is Perim) and the opposite point or volcanic peak called *J i b e l   S i j a n* . The larger of the two entrances is 11 miles wide, and the other only 1½. Strabo, Agathêmeros, and Pliny all agree

with the *Periplûs* in giving 60 stadia as the breadth of the straits. The first passage of those dreaded straits was regarded as a great achievement, and was naturally ascribed to Sesostris as the voyage though the straits of Kalpê was ascribed to Heraklês.

Situated on the shores of the straits was a place called *O k ê - l i s*. This was not a mart of commerce, but merely a bay with good anchorage and well supplied with water. It is identical with the modern Ghalla or Cella, which has a bay immediately within the straits. Strabo following Artemidoros notes here a promontory called *A k i l a*. Pliny (VI. xxxii. 157) mentions an emporium of the same name "ex quo in Indiam navigatur." In xxvi., 104 of the same Book he says: "Indos petentibus utilissimum est ab *O c e l i* egredi." Ptolemy mentions a *P s e u d o k ê l i s*, which he places at the distance of half a degree from the emporium of *O k ê l i s*.

26. Beyond O k ê l i s, the sea again widening out towards the east, and gradually expanding into the open main, there lies, at about the distance of 1,200 stadia, E u d a i m ô n   A r a b i a, a maritime village subject to that kingdom of which Kharibaêl is sovereign—a place with good anchorage, and supplied with sweeter and better water than that of Okêlis, and standing at the entrance of a bay where the land begins to retire inwards. It was called Eudaimôn ('rich and prosperous'), because in bygone days, when the merchants from India did not proceed to Egypt, and those from Egypt did not venture to cross over to the marts further east, but both came only as far as this city, it formed the common centre of their commerce, as Alexandria receives the wares which pass to and fro between Egypt and the ports of the Mediterranean. Now, however, it lies in ruins, the Emperor having destroyed it not long before our own times.

(26) At a distance beyond *O k ê l i s* of 1,200 stadia is the port of *E u d a i m ô n   A r a b i a*, which beyond doubt corresponds to *' Â d e n*, [lat. 12° 45′ N., long. 45° 21′ E.] now so well-known as the great packet station between Suez and India. The opinion held by some that Aden is the Eden mentioned by the Prophet Ezekiel (xxvii. 23) is opposed by Ritter and Winer. It is not mentioned by Pliny, though it has been erroneously held that the *A t t a n a e*, which he mentions in the following passage, was Aden. "Homnae et Attanae (v. 1. Athanae) quæ nunc oppida maxima celebrari a Persico mari negotiatores dicunt." (vi. 32.) Ptolemy, who calls it simply *A r a b i a*, speaks of it as an emporium, and places after it at the distance of a degree and a half *M e l a n   H o r o s*, or Black Hill, 17 miles from the coast, which is in long. 46° 59′ E. The place, as the *Periplûs* informs us, received the name of *E u d a i m ô n* from the great prosperity and wealth which it derived from being the great entrepôt of the trade between India and Egypt. It was in decay when that work was written, but even in the time of Ptolemy had begun to show symptoms of returning prosperity, and in the time of Constantine it was known as the 'Roman Emporium,' and

had almost regained its former consequence, as is gathered from a passage in the works of the ecclesiastical historian Philostorgios. It is thus spoken of by Edrisi (I. p. 51): "'*Â d e n* is a small town, but renowned for its seaport whence ships depart that are destined for Sind, India, and China." In the middle ages it became again the centre of the trade between India and the Red Sea, and thus regained that wonderful prosperity which in the outset had given it its name. In this flourishing condition it was found by Marco Polo, whose account of its wealth, power and influence is, as Vincent remarks, almost as magnificent as that which Agatharkhidês attributed to the Sabæans in the time of the Ptolemies, when the trade was carried on in the same manner. Agatharkhidês does not however mention the place by name, but it was probably the city which he describes without naming it as lying on the White Sea without the straits, whence, he says, the Sabæans sent out colonies or factories into India, and where the fleets from Persis, Karmania and the Indus arrived. The name of *A d e n* is supposed to be a corruption from *E u d a i m ô n*.

27. To *E u d a i m ô n   A r a b i a* at once succeeds a great length of coast and a bay extending 2,000 stadia or more, inhabited by nomadic tribes and Ikhthyophagoi settled in villages. On doubling a cape which projects from it you come to another trading seaport, *K a n ê*, which is subject to *E l e a z o s*, king of the incense country. Two barren islands lie opposite to it, 120 stadia off—one called *O r n e ô n*, and the other *T r o u l l a s*. At some distance inland from *K a n ê* is *S a b b a t h a*, the principal city of the district, where the king resides. At *K a n ê* is collected all the incense that is produced in the country, this being conveyed to it partly on camels, and partly *by sea* on floats supported on inflated skins, a local invention, and also in boats. *K a n ê* carries on trade with ports across the ocean—*B a r u g a z a*, *S k y t h i a*, and *O m a n a*, and the adjacent coast of *P e r s i s*.

(27) The coast beyond Aden is possessed partly by wandering tribes, and partly by tribes settled in villages which subsist on fish. Here occurs a bay—that now called Ghubhet-al-Kamar, which extends upwards of 2,000 stadia, and ends in a promontory—that now called Râs-al-Asîdah or Bâ-l-hâf [lat. 13° 58′ N., long 48° 9′ S.—a cape with a hill near the fishing village of Gillah]. Beyond this lies another great mart called *K a n ê*. It is mentioned by Pliny, and also by Ptolemy, who assigns it a position in agreement with the indications given in the *Periplûs*. It has been identified with the port now called Hisn Ghorâb [lat. 14° 0′ N. long. 48° 19′ E.]. Not far from this is an island called Halanî, which answers to the *T r o u l l a s* of our author. Further south is another island, which is called by the natives of the adjacent coast *S i k k a h*, but by sailors Jibûs. This is covered with the dung of birds which in countless multitudes have always frequented it, and may be therefore identified with the *O r n e ô n* of the *Periplûs*. *K a n ê* was subject

to Eleazos, the king of the Frankincense Country, who resided at *Sabbatha*, or as it is called by Pliny (VI. xxxii. 155) *Sabota*, the capital of the Atramitae or Adramitae, a tribe of Sabæans from whom the division of Arabia now known as Hadhramaut takes its name. The position of this city cannot be determined with certainty. Wellsted, who proceeded into the interior from the coast near Hisn Ghorab through Wadi Meifah, came after a day's journey and a half to a place called Nakb-el-Hajar, situated in a highly cultivated district, where he found ruins of an ancient city of the Himyarites crowning an eminence that rose gently with a double summit from the fertile plain. The city appeared to have been built in the most solid style of architecture, and to have been protected by a very lofty wall formed of square blocks of black marble, while the inscriptions plainly betokened that it was an old seat of the Himyarites. A close similarity could be traced between its ruins and those of *Kanê*, to which there was an easy communication by the valley of *Meifah*. This place, however, can hardly be regarded as *Sabbatha* without setting aside the distances given by Ptolemy, and Wellsted moreover learned from the natives that other ruins of a city of not less size were to be met with near a village called Esan, which could be reached by a three days' journey. — (See Haines, *Mem. of the S. Coast of Arab.*)

28. From Egypt it imports, like Mouza, corn and a little wheat, cloths for the Arabian market, both of the common sort and the plain, and large quantities of a sort that is adulterated; also copper, tin, coral, styrax, and all the other articles enumerated at Mouza. Besides these there are brought also, principally for the king, wrought silver plate, and specie as well as horses and carved images, and plain cloth of a superior quality. Its exports are its indigenous products, frankincense and aloes, and such commodities as it shares in common with other marts on the same coast. Ships sail for this port at the same season of the year as those bound for Mouza, but earlier.

(28) With regard to the staple product of this region — frankincense, the *Periplûs* informs us that it was brought for exportation to *Kanê*. It was however in the first place, if we may credit Pliny, conveyed to the Metropolis. He says (xv. 32) that when gathered it was carried into *Sabota* on camels which could enter the city only by one particular gate, and that to take it by any other route was a crime punished by death. The priests, he adds, take a tithe for a deity named *Sabis*, and that until this impost is paid, the article cannot be sold.

Some writers would identify *Sabbatha* with *Mariabo* (Marab), but on insufficient grounds. It has also been conjectured that the name may be a lengthened form of *Saba* (Sheba), a common appellation for cities in Arabia Felix. [Müller places Sabbatha at Sawa, lat. 16° 13′ N., long. 48° 9′ E.]

29. As you proceed from K a n ê the land retires more and more, and there succeeds another very deep and far-stretching gulf, S a k h a l i t ê s by name, and also the frankincense country, which is mountainous and difficult of access, having a dense air loaded with vapours [and] the frankincense exhaled from the trees. These trees, which are not of any great size or height, yield their incense in the form of a concretion on the bark, just as several of our trees in Egypt exude gum. The incense is collected by the hand of the king's slaves, and malefactors condemned to this service as a punishment. The country is unhealthy in the extreme:—pestilential even to those who sail along the coast, and mortal to the poor wretches who gather the incense, who also suffer from lack of food, which readily cuts them off.

(29) The next place mentioned by our author after *K a n ê* is a Bay called *S a k h a l î t e s*, which terminates at *S u a g r o s*, a promontory which looks eastward, and is the greatest cape in the whole world. There was much difference of opinion among the ancient geographers regarding the position of this Bay, and consequently regarding that of Cape *S u a g r o s*.

30. Now at this gulf is a promontory, the greatest in the world, looking towards the east, and called S u a g r o s, at which is a fortress which protects the country, and a harbour, and a magazine to which the frankincense which is collected is brought. Out in the open sea, facing this promontory, and lying between it and the promontory of A r ô m a t a, which projects from the opposite coast, though nearer to S u a g r o s, is the island going by the name of D i o s k o r i d ê s, which is of great extent, but desert and very moist, having rivers and crocodiles and a great many vipers, and lizards of enormous size, of which the flesh serves for food, while the grease is melted down and used as a substitute for oil. This island does not, however, produce either the grape or corn. The population, which is but scanty, inhabits the north side of the island—that part of it which looks towards the mainland (*of Arabia*). It consists of an intermixture of foreigners, Arabs, Indians, and even Greeks, who resort hither for the purposes of commerce. The island produces the tortoise,—the genuine, the land, and the white sort: the latter very abundant, and distinguished for the largeness of its shell; also the mountain sort which is of extraordinary size and has a very thick shell, whereof the underpart cannot be used, being too hard to cut, while the serviceable part is made into moneyboxes, tablets, escritoires, and ornamental articles of that description. It yields also the vegetable dye (κιννάβαρι) called Indicum (or Dragon's-blood), which is gathered as it distils from trees.

(30) Some would identify the latter with Ras-el-Had, and others on account of the similarity of the name with Cape *S a u g r a* or *S a u k i r a h* [lat. 18° 8′ N., long. 56° 35′ E.], where Ptolemy places a city *S u a g r o s* at a distance of 6 degrees from *K a n ê*, But *S u a g r o s* is undoubtedly Ras Fartak [lat. 15° 39′ N., long 52° 15′ E.], which is at a distance of 4 degrees from *H i s n G h o r a b*, or *K a n ê*, and which, rising to the height of 2,500 feet on a coast which is all low-lying, is a very conspicuous object, said to be discernible from a distance of 60 miles out at sea. Eighteen miles west

from this promontory is a village called Saghar, a name which might probably have suggested to the Greeks that of *S u a g r o s*. Consistent with this identification is the passage of Pliny (VI. 32) where he speaks of the island *D i o s c o r i d i s* (Sokotra) as distant from *S u a g r o s*, which he calls the utmost projection of the coast, 2,240 stadia or 280 miles, which is only about 30 miles in excess of the real distance, 2,000 stadia.

With regard to the position of the Bay of Sakhalitês, Ptolemy, followed by Marcianus, places it to the East of Suagros. Marinos on the other hand, like the *Periplûs*, places it to the west of it. Muller agrees with Fresnel in regarding *S a k h l ê*, mentioned by Ptolemy (VI. vii. 41) as 1½ degree East of Makalleh [lat. 14° 31′ N., long 49° 7′ W.] as the same with Shehr—which is now the name of all that mountainous region extending from the seaport of Makalleh to the bay in which lie the islands of Kurya Murya. He therefore takes this to be in the Regio Sakhalîtês, and rejects the opinion of Ptolemy as inconsistent with this determination. With regard to Shehr or Shehar [lat. 14° 38′ N., long. 49° 22′ E.] Yule (*M. Polo*, II. vol. p. 440, note) says: "Shihr or Shehr still exists on the Arabian Coast as a town and district about 330 miles east of Aden." The name Shehr in some of the oriental geographies includes the whole Coast up to Oman. The hills of the Shehr and Dhafâr districts were the great source of produce of the Arabian frankincense.

The island of *D i o s k o r i d ê s* (now Sokotra) is placed by the *Periplûs* nearer to Cape *S u a g r o s* than to Cape *A r ô m a t a* —although its distance from the former is nearly double the distance from the latter. The name, though in appearance a Greek one, is in reality of Sanskrit origin; from *Dvîpa Sukhâdâra*, i.e. *insula fortunata*, 'Island abode of Bliss.' The accuracy of the statements made regarding it in the *Periplûs* is fully confirmed by the accounts given of it by subsequent writers. Kosmas, who wrote in the 6th century, says that the inhabitants spoke Greek, and that he met with people from it who were on their way to Ethiopia, and that they spoke Greek. "The ecclesiastical historian Nikephoros Kallistos," says Yule, "seems to allude to the people of Sokotra when he says that among the nations visited by the Missionary Theophilus in the time of Constantius, were 'the Assyrians on the verge of the outer Ocean, towards the East ... whom Alexander the Great, after driving them from Syria, sent thither to settle, and to this day they keep their mother tongue, though all of the blackest, through the power of the sun's rays.' The Arab voyagers of the 9th century say that the island was colonized with Greeks by Alexander the Great, in order to promote the culture of the Sokotrine aloes; when the other Greeks adopted Christianity these did likewise, and they had continued to retain their profession of it. The colonizing by Alexander is probably a fable, but invented to account for facts." (*Marco Polo* II. 401.) The aloe, it may be noted, is not mentioned in the *Periplûs* as one of the products of the island. The islanders, though at one time Christians, are now Muhammadans, and subject as of yore to Arabia. The people of the interior are still of distinct race with curly hair, Indian complexion, and regular features. The coast people are mongrels of Arab and mixed descent. Probably in old times civilization and Greek may have been confined to the littoral foreigners. Marco Polo notes that so far back as the 10th century it was one of the stations frequented by the Indian corsairs called *B a w â r i j*, belonging to Kachh and Gujarat.

31. The island is subject to the king of the frankincense country, in the same way as A z a n i a is subject to Kharibaël and the despot of M o p h a r i t i s. It used to be visited by some (*merchants*) from Mouza, and others on the homeward voyage from Limurikê and Barugaza would occasionally touch at it, importing rice, corn, Indian cotton and female-slaves, who, being rare, always commanded a ready market. In exchange for these commodities they would receive as fresh cargo great quantities of tortoise-shell. The revenues of the island are at the present day farmed out by its sovereigns, who, however, maintain a garrison in it for the protection of their interests.

32. Immediately after S u a g r o s follows a gulf deeply indenting the mainland of O m a n a , and having a width of 600 stadia. Beyond it are high mountains, rocky and precipitous, and inhabited by men who live in caves. The range extends onward for 500 stadia, and beyond where it terminates lies an important harbour called M o s k h a , the appointed port to which the *Sakhalitik* frankincense is forwarded. It is regularly frequented by a number of ships from Kanê; and such ships as come from Limurikê and Barugaza too late in the season put into harbour here for the winter, where they dispose of their muslins, corn, and oil to the king's officers, receiving in exchange frankincense, which lies in piles throughout the whole of S a k h a l i t i s without a guard to protect it, as if the locality were indebted to some divine power for its security. Indeed, it is impossible to procure a cargo, either publicly or by connivance, without the king's permission. Should one take furtively on board were it but a single grain, his vessel can by no possibility escape from harbour.

(32) Returning to the mainland the narrative conducts us next to *M o s k h a* , a seaport trading with *K a n ê* , and a wintering place for vessels arriving late in the season from Malabar and the Gulf of Khambât. The distance of this place from Suagros is set down at upwards of 1,100 stadia, 600 of which represent the breadth of a bay which begins at the Cape, and is called *O m a n a   A l - K a - m a r* . The occurrence of the two names Omana and Moskha in such close connexion led D'Anville to suppose that *M o s k h a* is identical with *M a s k a t* , the capital of *O m a n* , the country lying at the south-east extremity of Arabia, and hence that Ras-el-Ḥad,

beyond which Maskat lies, must be Cape Suagros. This supposition is, however, untenable, since the identification of Moskha with the modern *A u s e r a* is complete. For, in the first place, the Bay of Seger, which begins at Cape Fartak, is of exactly the same measurement across to Cape Thurbot Ali as the Bay of *O m a - n a*, and again the distance from Cape Thurbot Ali [lat. 16° 38′ N., long. 53° 3′ E.] to Ras-al-Sair, the *A u s a r a* of Ptolemy, corresponds almost as exactly to the distance assigned by our author from the same Cape to *M o s k h a*. Moreover Pliny (XII. 35) notices that one particular kind of incense bore the name of *Ausaritis*, and, as the *Periplûs* states that *M o s k h a* was the great emporium of the incense trade, the identification is satisfactory.

There was another Moskha on this coast which was also a port. It lay to the west of Suagros, and has been identified with *K o s h î n* [lat. 15° 21′ N. long. 51° 39′ E.]. Our author, though correct in his description of the coast, may perhaps have erred in his nomenclature; and this is the more likely to have happened as it scarcely admits of doubt that he had no personal knowledge of South Arabia beyond *K a n ê* and Cape *S u a g r o s*. Besides no other author speaks of an Omana so far to westward as the position assigned to the Bay of that name. The tract immediately beyond *M o s k h a* or Ausera is low and fertile, and is called *D o f a r* or *Z h a f â r*, after a famous city now destroyed, but whose ruins are still to be traced between Al-hâfâh and Addahariz. "This Dhafâr," says Yule (*Marco Polo* II. p. 442 note) "or the bold fountain above it, is supposed to be the *S e p h a r* of *Genesis* X. 30." It is certain that the Himyarites had spread their dominion as far eastward as this place. Marco Polo thus describes Dhafâr:—"It stands upon the sea, and has a very good haven, so that there is a great traffic of shipping between this and India; and the merchants take hence great numbers of Arab horses to that market, making great profits thereby.... Much white incense is produced here, and I will tell you how it grows. The trees are like small fir-trees; these are notched with a knife in several places, and from these notches the incense is exuded. Sometimes, also, it flows from the tree without any notch, this is by reason of the great heat of the sun there." Müller would identify *M o s k h a* with Zhafâr, and accounts for the discrepancy of designation by supposing that our author had confounded the name *M a s k a t*, which was the great seat of the traffic in frankincense with the name of the greatest city in the district which actually produced it. A similar confusion he thinks transferred the name of Oman to the same part of the country. The climate of the incense country is described as being extremely unhealthy, but its unhealthiness seems to have been designedly exaggerated.

33. From the port of M o s k h a onward to A s i k h , a distance of about 1,500 stadia, runs a range of hills pretty close to the shore, and at its termination there are seven islands bearing the name of Z e n o b i o s , beyond which again we come to another barbarous district not subject to any power in Arabia, but to Persia. If when sailing by this coast you stand well out to sea so as to keep a direct course, then at about a distance from the island of Z e n o b i o s of 2,000 stadia you arrive at another island, called that of S a r a p i s , lying off shore, say, 120 stadia. It is about 200 stadia broad and 600 long, possessing three villages inhabited by a *savage* tribe of I k h t h y o p h a g o i , who speak the Arabic language, and whose clothing consists of a girdle made from the leaves of the cocoa-palm. The island produces in great plenty tortoise of excellent quality, and the merchants of K a n ê accordingly fit out little boats and cargo-ships to trade with it.

(33) Beyond *M o s k h a* the coast is mountainous as far as *A s i k h* and the islands of Zenobios—a distance excessively estimated at 1,500 stadia. The mountains referred to are 5,000 feet in height, and are those now called Subaha. *A s i k h* is readily to be identified with the *H â s e k* of Arabian geographers. Edrisi (I. p. 54) says: "Thence (from Marbat) to the town of Hâsek is a four days' journey and a two days' sail. Before *H â s e k* are the two islands of *K h a r t a n* and *M a r t a n* . Above *H â s e k* is a high mountain named *S o u s* , which commands the sea. It is an inconsiderable town but populous." This place is now in ruins, but has left its name to the promontory on which it stood [Râs Hâsek, lat. 17° 23′ N. long. 55° 20′ E. opposite the island of Hasiki]. The islands of *Z e n o b i o s* are mentioned by Ptolemy as seven in number, and are those called by Edrisi *K h a r t a n* and *M a r t a n* , now known as the *K u r i y â n M u r i y â n* islands. The inhabitants belonged to an Arab tribe which was spread from Hâsek to Râs-el-Ḥad, and was called *B e i t* or *B e n i J e n a b i* , whence the Greek name. M. Polo in the 31st chapter of his travels "discourseth of the two islands called Male and Female," the position of which he vaguely indicates by saying that "when you leave the kingdom of *K e s - m a c o r a n* (Mekran) which is on the mainland, you go by sea some 500 miles towards the south, and then you find the 2 islands Male and Female lying about 30 miles distant from one another." (See also *Marco Polo*, vol. II. p. 396 note.)

Beyond *A s i k h* is a district inhabited by barbarians, and subject not to Arabia but to Persis. Then succeeds at a distance of 200 stadia beyond the islands of *Z e n o b i o s* the island of *S a r a p i s* , (the Ogyris of Pliny) now called Masira [lat. 20° 10′ to 20° 42′ N., long. 58° 37′ to 58° 59′ E.] opposite that part of the coast where Oman now begins. The *Periplûs* exaggerates both its breadth and its distance from the continent. It was still inhabited by a tribe of fish-eaters in the time of Ebn Batuta, by whom it was visited.

On proceeding from *S a r a p i s* the adjacent coast bends

round, and the direction of the voyage changes to north. The great cape which forms the south-eastern extremity of Arabia called *Ras-el-Had* [lat. 22° 33′ N. long. 59° 48′ E.] is here indicated, but without being named; Ptolemy calls it *Korodamon* (VI. vii. 11.)

34. If sailing onward you wind round with the adjacent coast to the north, then as you approach the entrance of the Persian Gulf you fall in with a group of islands which lie in a range along the coast for 2,000 stadia, and are called the islands of K a l a i o u. The inhabitants of the adjacent coast are cruel and treacherous, and see imperfectly in the daytime.

(34) Beyond it, and near the entrance to the Persian Gulf, occurs, according to the *Periplûs*, a group of many islands, which lie in a range along the coast over a space of 2,000 stadia, and are called the islands of K a l a i o u. Here our author is obviously in error, for there are but three groups of islands on this coast, which are not by any means near the entrance of the Gulf. They lie beyond Maskat [lat. 23° 38′ N. long. 58° 36′ E.] and extend for a considerable distance along the Batinah coast. The central group is that of the Deymâniyeh islands (probably the Damnia of Pliny) which are seven in number, and lie nearly opposite Birkeh [lat 23° 42′ N. long. 57° 55′ E.]. The error, as Müller suggests, may be accounted for by supposing that the tract of country called El Baṭinah was mistaken for islands. This tract, which is very low and extremely fertile, stretches from Birkeh [lat. 23° 42′ N. long. 57° 55′ E.] onward to Jibba, where high mountains approach the very shore, and run on in an unbroken chain to the mouth of the Persian Gulf. The islands are not mentioned by any other author, for the *C a l a c o u   i n s u l a e* of Pliny (VI. xxxii. 150) must, to avoid utter confusion, be referred to the coast of the Arabian Gulf. There is a place called *E l   K i l a t*, the Akilla of Pliny [lat. 22° 40′ N. long. 59° 24′ E.]—but whether this is connected with the *K a l a i o u* islands of the *Periplûs* is uncertain [Conf. *Ind. Ant.* vol. IV. p. 48. El Kilhat, south of Maskat and close to Ṣûr, was once a great port.]

35. Near the last headland of the islands of K a l a i o u is the mountain called K a l o n (Pulcher),[20] to which succeeds, at no great distance, the mouth of the Persian Gulf, where there are very many pearl fisheries. On the left of the entrance, towering to a vast height, are the mountains which bear the name of A s a b o i, and directly opposite on the right you see another mountain high and round, called the hill of S e m i r a m i s. The strait which separates them has a width of 600 stadia, and through this opening the Persian Gulf pours its vast expanse of waters far up into the interior. At the very head of this gulf there is a regular mart of commerce, called the city of A p o l o g o s, situate near P a s i n o u - K h a r a x

[20] "This" (Mons Pulcher) says Major-General Miles, "is Jebel Lahrim or Shaum, the loftiest and most conspicuous peak on the whole cape (Mussendom), being nearly 7,000 feet high." —*Jour. R. As. Soc.* (N.S.) vol. X. p. 168.—ED.

and the river Euphrates.

(35) Before the mouth of the Persian Gulf is reached occurs a height called *K a l o n* (Fair Mount) at the last head of the islands of Papias—τῶν Παπίου νήσων. This reading has been altered by Fabricius and Schwanbeck to των Καλαιου νησων. The Fair Mount, according to Vincent, would answer sufficiently to Cape Fillam, if that be high land, and not far from Fillam are the straits. The great cape which Arabia protrudes at these straits towards Karmania is now called Ras Mussendom. It was seen from the opposite coast by the expedition under Nearkhos, to whom it appeared to be a day's sail distant. The height on that coast is called Semiramis, and also Strongylê from its round shape. Mussendom, the 'Asabôn akron' of Ptolemy, Vincent says, "is a sort of Lizard Point to the Gulf; for all the Arabian ships take their departure from it with some ceremonies of superstition, imploring a blessing on their voyage, and setting afloat a toy like a vessel rigged and decorated, which if it is dashed to pieces by the rocks is to be accepted by the ocean as an offering for the escape of the vessel." [The straits between the island of Mussendom and the mainland are called El Bab, and this is the origin of the name of the Papiæ islands.—Miles' *Jour. R. A. Soc.* N. S. vol. x. p. 168.]

The actual width of the straits is 40 miles. Pliny gives it at 50, and the *Periplûs* at 75. Cape Mussendom is represented in the *Periplûs* as in Ptolemy by the Mountains of the Asabi which are described as tremendous heights, black, grim, and abrupt. They are named from the tribe of *B e n i   A s a b*.

We enter now the Gulf itself, and here the *Periplûs* mentions only two particulars: the famous Pearl Fisheries which begin at the straits and extend to Bahrein, and the situation of a regular trading mart called *A p o l o g o s*, which lies at the very head of the Gulf on the Euphrates, and in the vicinity of *S p a s i n o u K h a r a x*. This place does not appear to be referred to in any other classical work, but it is frequently mentioned by Arabian writers under the name of Oboleh or Obolegh. As an emporium it took the place of *T e r ê d ô n* or *D i r i d ô t i s*, just as *B a s r a* (below which it was situated) under the second Khaliphate took the place of *O b o l e h* itself. According to Vincent, Oboleh, or a village that represents it, still exists between Basra and the Euphrates. The canal also is called the canal of Oboleh. *K h a r a x   P a s i n o u* was situated where the *K a r û n* (the *E u l æ u s* of the ancients) flows into the *P a s i t i g r i s*, and is represented by the modern trading town *M u h a m m a r a h*. It was founded by Alexander the Great, and after its destruction, was rebuilt by Antiokhos Epiphanes, who changed its name from Alexandreia to Antiokheia. It was afterwards occupied by an Arab Chief called Pasines, or rather *Spasines*, who gave it the name by which it is best known. Pliny states that the original town was only 10 miles from the sea, but that in his time the existing place was so much as 120 miles from it. It was the birth-place of two eminent geographers—Dionysius Periegetes and Isidôros.

36. If you coast along the mouth of the gulf you are conducted by a six days' voyage to another seat of trade belonging to Persia, called O m a n a .[21] Barugaza maintains a regular commercial intercourse with both these Persian ports, despatching thither large vessels freighted with copper, sandalwood, beams for rafters, horn, and logs of sasamina and ebony. Omana imports also frankincense from Kanê, while it exports to Arabia a particular species of vessels called *madara*, which have their planks sewn together. But both from A p o l o g o s and O m a n a there are exported to Barugaza and to Arabia great quantities of pearl, of mean quality however compared with the Indian sort, together with purple, cloth for the natives, wine, dates in great quantity, and gold and slaves.

(36) After this cursory glance at the great gulf, our author returns to the straits, and at once conducts us to the Eastern shores of the æErythræan, where occurs another emporium belonging to Persis, at a distance from the straits of 6 courses or 3,000 stadia. This is Omana. It is mentioned by Pliny (VI. xxxii. 149) who makes it belong to Arabia, and accuses preceding writers for placing it in Karmania.

The name of *Omana* has been corrupted in the MSS. of Ptolemy into Nommana, Nombana, *Kommana*, Kombana, but Marcian has preserved the correct spelling. From Omana as from Apologos great quantities of pearl of an inferior sort were exported to Arabia and Barugaza. No part however of the produce of India is mentioned as among its exports, although it was the centre of commerce between that country and Arabia.

37. After leaving the district of O m a n a the country of the P a r s i d a i succeeds, which belongs to another government, and the bay which bears the name of T e r a b d o i , from the midst of which a cape projects. Here also is a river large enough to permit the entrance of ships, with a small mart at its mouth called O r a i a . Behind it in the interior, at the distance of a seven days' journey from the coast, is the city where the king resides, called Rhambakia. This district, in addition to corn, produces wine, rice, and dates, though in the tract near the sea, only

[21] "The city of Omana is Ṣoḥar, the ancient capital of Omana, which name, as is well known, it then bore, and Pliny is quite right in correcting *former writers* who had placed it in Caramania, on which coast there is no good evidence that there was a place of this name. Nearchus does not mention it, and though the author of the *Periplûs of the Erithræan Sea* does locate it in Persia, it is pretty evident he never visited the place himself, and he must have mistaken the information he obtained from others. It was this city of Ṣoḥar most probably that bore the appellation of Emporium Persarum, in which, as Philostorgius relates, permission was given to Theophilus, the ambassador of Constantine, to erect a Christian church." The Homna of Pliny may be a repetition of Omana or Ṣoḥar, which he had already mentioned.—Miles in *Jour. R. As. Soc.* (N. S.) vol. X. pp. 164-5.—ED.

the fragrant gum called bdellium.

(37) The district which succeeds Omana belongs to the *P a r - s i d a i*, a tribe in Gedrosia next neighbours to the *A r b i t a e* on the East. They are mentioned by Ptolemy (VI. xx., p. 439) and by Arrian (*Indika* xxvi.) who calls them *P a s i r e e s*, and notes that they had a small town called *P a s i r a*, distant about 60 stadia from the sea, and a harbour with good anchorage called *B a g i s - a r a*. The Promontory of the *Periplûs* is also noted and described as projecting far into the sea, and being high and precipitous. It is the Cape now called *A r a b a h* or *U r m a r a h*. The Bay into which it projects is called *T e r a b d ô n*, a name which is found only in our author. Vincent erroneously identifies this with the *P a r a g ô n* of Ptolemy. It is no doubt the Bay which extends from Cape Gua- del to Cape Monze. The river which enters this Bay, at the mouth of which stood the small mart called *O r a i a*, was probably that which is now called the Akbor. The royal city which lay inland from the sea a seven days' journey was perhaps, as Mannert has conjectured, *R a m b a k i a*, mentioned by Arrian (*Anab.* vi. 21) as the capital of the *O r e i t a i* or *H o r i t a i*.

38. After this region, where the coast is already deeply indented by gulfs caused by the land advancing with a vast curve from the east, succeeds the sea- board of Skythia, a region which extends to northward. It is very low and flat, and contains the mouths of the S i n t h o s (Indus), the largest of all the rivers which fall into the Erythræan Sea, and which, indeed, pours into it such a vast body of water that while you are yet far off from the land at its mouth you find the sea turned of a white colour by its waters.

The sign by which voyagers before sighting land know that it is near is their meeting with serpents floating on the water; but higher up and on the coasts of Persia the first sign of land is seeing them of a different kind, called *graai*. [Sansk. *graha*—an alligator.] The river has seven mouths, all shallow, marshy and un- fit for navigation except only the middle stream, on which is B a r b a r i k o n , a trading seaport. Before this town lies a small islet, and behind it in the interior is M i n n a g a r , the metropolis of Skythia, which is governed, however, by Parthian princes, who are perpetually at strife among themselves, expelling each the other.

(38) We now approach the mouths of the Indus which our author calls the *S i n t h o s*, transliterating the native name of it—*S i n d h u*. In his time the wide tract which was watered by this river in the lower part of its course was called *I n d o s k y - t h i a*. It derived its name from the Skythian tribes (the *Ś â k a* of Sansk.) who after the overthrow of the Graeco-Baktrian empire gradually passed southward to the coast, where they established themselves about the year 120 B. C., occupying all the region be- tween the Indus and the Narmadâ. They are called by Dionysios Periegetes *N o t i o i S k y t h a i*, the Southern Skythians. Our au- thor mentions two cities which belonged to them—*B a r b a r i k o n*

and *M i n n a g a r* ; the former of which was an emporium situated near the sea on the middle and only navigable branch of the Indus. Ptolemy has a *B a r b a r e i* in the Delta, but the position he assigns to it, does not correspond with that of *B a r b a r i k o n* . *M i n n a g a r* was the Skythian metropolis. It lay inland, on or near the banks of the Indus.

39. Ships accordingly anchor near B a r b a r i k ê , but all their cargoes are conveyed by the river up to the king, who resides in the metropolis.

The articles imported into this emporium are — Ἱματισμὸς ἁπλοῦς ἱκανὸς — Clothing, plain and in considerable quantity.

Ἱματισμὸς νόθος οὐ πολὺς — Clothing, mixed, not much.

Πολύμιτα — Flowered cottons.

Χρυσόλιθον — Yellow-stone, topazes.

Κοράλλιον — Coral.

Στύραξ — Storax.

Λίβανος — Frankincense (*Lôbân*).

Ὑαλᾶ σκεύη — Glass vessels.

Ἀργυρώματα — Silver plate.

Χρῆμα — Specie.

Οἶνος οὐ πολύς — Wine, but not much.

The exports are: —

Κόστος — Costus, a spice.

Βδέλλα — Bdellium, a gum.

Λύκιον — A yellow dye (*Ruzot*).

Νάρδος — Spikenard.

Λίθος καλλαϊνος — Emeralds or green-stones.

Σάπφειρος — Sapphires.

Σηρικὰ δέρματα — Furs from China.

Ὀθόνιον — Cottons.

Νῆμα Σηρικὸν — Silk thread.

Ἰνδικὸν μέλαν — Indigo.

Ships destined for this port put out to sea when the Indian monsoon prevails — that is, about the month of July or Epiphi. The voyage at this season is attended with danger, but being shorter is more expeditious.

(39) Ships did not go up to it but remained at *B a r b a r i k o n* , their cargoes being conveyed up the river in small boats. In Ptolemy (VII. i. 61) the form of the name is *B i n a g a r a* , which is less

correct since the word is composed of *Min*, the Indian name for the Skythians, and *nagar*, a city. Ritter considers that *Thaṭha* is its modern representative, since it is called *Saminagar* by the Jâḍejâ Rajputs who, though settled in Kachh, derive their origin from that city. To this view it is objected that Ṭhaṭha is not near the position which Ptolemy assigns to his *Binagara*. Mannert places it at *Bakkar*, D'Anville at *Mansura*, and Vincent at *Menhabery* mentioned by Edrisi (I. p. 164) as distant two stations or 60 miles from *Dabil*, which again was three stations or 90 miles from the mouth of the Indus, that is it lay at the head of the Delta. Our author informs us that in his time *Minagar* was ruled by Parthian princes. The Parthians (the Parada of Sanskrit writers) must therefore have subverted a Skythian dynasty which must have been that which (as Benfey has shown) was founded by *Yeukaotschin* between the years 30 and 20 B.C., or about 30 years only after the famous Indian Æra called *Śâkâbda* (the year of the Śâka) being that in which Vikramâditya expelled the Skythians from Indian soil. The statement of the *Periplûs* that Parthian rulers succeeded the Skythian is confirmed by Parthian coins found everywhere in this part of the country. These sovereigns must have been of consequence, or the trade of their country very lucrative to the merchant as appears by the presents necessary to ensure his protection—plate, musical instruments, handsome girls for the Harem, the best wine, plain cloth of high price, and the finest perfumes. The profits of the trade must therefore have been great, but if Pliny's account be true, that every pound laid out in India produced a hundred at Rome, greater exactions than these might easily have been supported.

40. After the river S i n t h o s is passed we reach another gulf, which cannot be easily seen. It has two divisions,—the Great and the Little by name,—both shoal with violent and continuous eddies extending far out from the shore, so that before ever land is in sight ships are often grounded on the shoals, or being caught within the eddies are lost. Over this gulf hangs a promontory which, curving from E i r i n o n first to the east, then to the south, and finally to the west, encompasses the gulf called B a r a k ê, in the bosom of which lie seven islands. Should a vessel approach the entrance of this gulf, the only chance of escape for those on board is at once to alter their course and stand out to sea, for it is all over with them if they are once fairly within the womb of B a r a k ê, which surges with vast and mighty billows, and where the sea, tossing in violent commotion, forms eddies and impetuous whirlpools in every direction. The bottom varies, presenting in places sudden shoals, in others being scabrous with jagged rocks, so that when an anchor grounds its cable is either at once cut through, or soon broken by friction at the bottom. The sign by which voyagers know they are approaching this bay is their seeing serpents floating about on the water, of extraordinary size and of a black colour, for those met with lower down and in the neighbourhood of Barugaza are of less size, and in colour green and golden.

(40) The first place mentioned after the Indus is the Gulf of *Eirinon*, a name of which traces remain in the modern appellation the *Raṇ* of Kachh. This is no longer covered with water except during the monsoon, when it is flooded by sea water or by rains and inundated rivers. At other seasons it is not even a marsh, for its bed is hard, dry and sandy; a mere saline waste almost entirely devoid of herbage, and frequented but by one quadruped—the wild ass. Burnes conjectured that its desiccation resulted from an upheaval of the earth caused by one of those earthquakes which are so common in that part of India. The *Raṇ* is connected with the Gulf of Kachh, which our author calls the Gulf of *Barakê*. His account of it is far from clear. Perhaps, as Müller suggests, he comprehended under *Eirinon* the interior portion of the Gulf of Kachh, limiting the Gulf of *Barakê* to the exterior portion or entrance to it. This gulf is called that of Kanthi by Ptolemy, who mentions *Barakê* only as an island, [and the south coast of Kachh is still known by the name of Kantha]. The islands of the *Periplûs* extend westward from the neighbourhood of *Navanagar* to the very entrance of the Gulf.

41. To the gulf of B a r a k ê succeeds that of B a r u g a z a and the mainland of A r i a k ê, a district which forms the frontier of the kingdom of M o m b a r o s and of all India. The interior part of it which borders on S k y t h i a is called A b e r i a, and its sea-board S u r a s t r ê n ê. It is a region which produces abundantly corn and rice and the oil of sesamum, butter, muslins and the coarser fabrics which are manufactured from Indian cotton. It has also numerous herds of cattle. The natives are men of large stature and coloured black. The metropolis of the district is M i n - n a g a r, from which cotton cloth is exported in great quantity to B a r u g a z a. In this part of the country there are preserved even to this very day memorials of the expedition of Alexander, old temples, foundations of camps, and large wells. The extent of this coast, reckoned from B a r b a r i k o n to the promontory called P a - p i k ê, near A s t a k a p r a, which is opposite B a r u g a z a, is 3,000 stadia.

(41) To *Barakê* succeeds the Gulf of *Barugaza* (Gulf of *Khambhât*) and the sea-board of the region called *Ariakê*. The reading of the MS. here ἡ πρῄὸς Ἀραβικῆς χώρας is considered corrupt. Müller substitutes ἡ ἤπειρος τῆς Ἀριακῆς χώρας, though Mannert and others prefer Λαρικῆς χώρας, relying on Ptolemy, who places *Ariakê* to the south of *Larikê*, and says that *Larikê* comprehends the peninsula (of Gujarât) Barugaza and the parts adjacent. As *Ariakê* was however previously mentioned in the *Periplûs* (sec. 14) in connexion with Barugaza, and is afterwards mentioned (sec. 54) as trading with Muziris, it must no doubt have been mentioned by the author in its proper place, which is here. [Bhagvanlâl Indraji Pandit has shewn reasons however for correcting the readings into Αβαρατικη, the Prakrit form of *Aparântikâ*, an old name of the western sea board

of India.—*Ind. Ant.* vol. VII., pp. 259, 263.] Regarding the name *Larikê*, Yule has the following note (*Travels of M. Polo* vol. II., p. 353):—"*Lâr-Deśa*, the country of Lar," properly Lât-deśa, was an early name for the territory of Gujrat and the northern Konkan, embracing Saimur (the modern Chaul as I believe) Thaṇa, and Bharoch. It appears in Ptolemy in the form *Larikê*. The sea to the west of that coast was in the early Muhammadan times called the sea of Lâr, and the language spoken on its shores is called by *Mas'udi, Lâri*. Abulfeda's authority, Ibn Said, speaks of Lâr and Gujarât as identical.

Ariakê (Aparântikâ), our author informs us, was the beginning or frontier of India. That part of the interior of Ariakê which bordered on Skythia was called *Aberia* or Abiria (in the MS. erroneously Ibêria). The corresponding Indian word is *Abhira*, which designated the district near the mouths of the river. Having been even in very early times a great seat of commerce, some (as Lassen) have been led to think from a certain similarity of the names that this was the *Ophir* of scripture, a view opposed by Ritter. Abiria is mentioned by Ptolemy, who took it to be not a part of India but of Indoskythia. The sea-board of Ariakê was called *Surastrênê*, and is mentioned by Ptolemy, who says (VII. i. 55) it was the region about the mouths of the Indus and the Gulf of Kanthi. It answers to the Sanskrit *Surâshṭra*. Its capital was Minnagar,—a city which, as its name shows, had once belonged to the Min or Skythians. It was different of course from the Minnagar already mentioned as the capital of Indo-Skythia. It was situated to the south of *Ozênê* (Ujjayinî, or Ujjain), and on the road which led from that city to the River Narmadâ, probably near where Indôr now stands. It must have been the capital only for a short time, as Ptolemy informs us (II. i. 63) that *Ozênê* was in his time the capital of *Tiashanes* [probably the Chashṭana of Coins and the Cave Temple inscriptions]. From both places a great variety of merchandise was sent down the Narmadâ to Barugaza.

The next place our author mentions is a promontory called *Papikê* projecting into the Gulf of Khambât from that part of the peninsula of Gujarât which lies opposite to the Barugaza coast. Its distance from Barbarikon on the middle mouth of the Indus is correctly given at 3,000 stadia. This promontory is said to be near *Astakapra*, a place which is mentioned also by Ptolemy, and which (*Ind. Ant.* vol. V. p. 314) has been identified by Colonel Yule with *Hastakavapra* (now *Hâthab* near Bhaunagar), a name which occurs in a copper-plate grant of Dhruvasena I of Valabhi. With regard to the Greek form of this name Dr. Bühler thinks it is not derived immediately from the Sanskrit, but from an intermediate old Prakrit word Hastakampra, which had been formed by the contraction of the syllables *ava* to *â*, and the insertion of a nasal, according to the habits of the Gujarâtîs. The loss of the initial, he adds, may be explained by the difficulty which Gujarâtîs have now and probably had 1,600 years ago in pronouncing the spirans in its proper place. The modern name Hâthab or Hâthap may be a corruption of the shorter Sanskrit form Hastavapra.

42. After Papikê there is another gulf, exposed to the violence of the waves and running up to the north. Near its mouth is an island called B a i ô n ê s, and at its very head it receives a vast river called the M a i s. Those bound for B a r u g a z a sail up this gulf (which has a breadth of about 300 stadia), leaving the island on the left till it is scarcely visible in the horizon, when they shape their course east for the mouth of the river that leads to Barugaza. This is called the N a m n a d i o s.

> (42) Beyond *P a p i k ê*, we are next informed, there is another gulf running northward into the interior of the country. This is not really another Gulf but only the northern portion of the Gulf of Khambât, which the *Periplûs* calls the Gulf of Barugaza. It receives a great river, the *M a i s*, which is easily identified with the *M a h i*, and contains an island called *B a i ô n ê s* [the modern Peram], which you leave on the left hand as you cross over from Astakapra to Barugaza.

> We are now conducted to *B a r u g a z a*, the greatest seat of commerce in Western India, situated on a river called in the MS. of the *Periplûs* the *L a m n a i o s*, which is no doubt an erroneous reading for *N a m a d o s*, or Namnados or Namnadios. This river is the *N a r m a d â*. It is called by Ptolemy the Namades.

43. The passage into the gulf of B a r u g a z a is narrow and difficult of access to those approaching it from the sea, for they are carried either to the right or to the left, the left being the better passage of the two. On the right, at the very entrance of the gulf, lies a narrow stripe of shoal, rough and beset with rocks. It is called H e r ô n ê, and lies opposite the village of K a m m ô n i. On the left side right against this is the promontory of P a p i k ê, which lies in front of A s t a k a p r a, where it is difficult to anchor, from the strength of the current and because the cables are cut through by the sharp rocks at the bottom. But even if the passage into the gulf is secured the mouth of the Barugaza river is not easy to hit, since the coast is low and there are no certain marks to be seen until you are close upon them. Neither, if it is discovered, is it easy to enter, from the presence of shoals at the mouth of the river.

> (43) *B a r u g a z a* (Bharoch) which was 30 miles distant from its mouth, was both difficult and dangerous of access; for the entrance to the Gulf itself was, on the right, beset with a perilous stripe (*tainia*) of rocky shoal called *H e r ô n ê*, and on the left, (which was the safer course,) the violent currents which swept round the promontory of Papikê rendered it unsafe to approach the shore or to cast anchor. The shoal of Herônê was opposite a

village on the mainland called *K a m m ô n i*, the Kamanê of Ptolemy (VII. i.), who however places it to the north of the river's
mouth. Again, it was not only difficult to hit the mouth of the
river, but its navigation was endangered by sandbanks and the
violence of the tides, especially the high tide called the 'Bore,' of
which our author gives a description so particular and so vivid as
suffices to show that he was describing what he had seen with his
own eyes, and seen moreover for the first time. With regard to the
name *B a r u g a z a* the following passage, which I quote from Dr.
Wilson's *Indian Castes* (vol. II. p. 113) will elucidate its etymology:—"The *B h â r g a v a s* derive their designation from *B h a r g a -
v a*, the adjective form of *B h ṛ i g u*, the name of one of the ancient
Ṛishis. Their chief habitat is the district of Bharoch, which must
have got its name from a colony of the school of Bhṛigu having
been early established in this Kshêtra, probably granted to them
by some conqueror of the district. In the name *B a r u g a z a* given
to it by Ptolemy, we have a Greek corruption of Bhṛigukshêtra
(the territory of Bhṛigu) or Bhṛigukachha (the tongueland of
Bhṛigu)." Speaking of the Bhârgavas Dr. Drummond, in his *Gram-
matical Illustrations*, says:—"These Brâhmans are indeed poor and
ignorant. Many of them, and other illiterate Gujarâtîs, would, in
attempting to articulate Bhṛigushêtra, lose the half in coalesence,
and call it Bargacha, whence the Greeks, having no *Ch*, wrote it
Barugaza."

44. For this reason native fishermen appointed by Government are stationed
with well-manned long boats called *trappaga* and *kotumba* at the entrance of the
river, whence they go out as far as S u r a s t r ê n ê to meet ships, and pilot them
up to Barugaza. At the head of the gulf the pilot, immediately on taking charge of
a ship, with the help of his own boat's crew, shifts her head to keep her clear of the
shoals, and tows her from one fixed station to another, moving with the beginning
of the tide, and dropping anchor at certain roadsteads and basins when it ebbs.
These basins occur at points where the river is deeper than usual, all the way up
to B a r u g a z a, which is 300 stadia distant from the mouth of the river if you sail
up the stream to reach it.

45. India has everywhere a great abundance of rivers, and her seas ebb and
flow with tides of extraordinary strength, which increase with the moon, both
when new and when full, and for three days after each, but fall off in the intermediate space. About B a r u g a z a they are more violent than elsewhere; so that all
of a sudden you see the depths laid bare, and portions of the land turned into sea,
and the sea, where ships were sailing but just before, turned without warning into
dry land. The rivers, again, on the access of flood tide rushing into their channels
with the whole body of the sea, are driven upwards against their natural course for
a great number of miles with a force that is irresistible.

46. This is the reason why ships frequenting this emporium are exposed, both
in coming and going, to great risk, if handled by those who are unacquainted with

the navigation of the gulf or visit it for the first time, since the impetuosity of the tide when it becomes full, having nothing to stem or slacken it, is such that anchors cannot hold against it. Large vessels, moreover, if caught in it are driven athwart from their course by the rapidity of the current till they are stranded on shoals and wrecked, while the smaller craft are capsized, and many that have taken refuge in the side channels, being left dry by the receding tide, turn over on one side, and, if not set erect on props, are filled upon the return of the tide with the very first head of the flood, and sunk. But at new moons, especially when they occur in conjunction with a night tide, the flood sets in with such extraordinary violence that on its beginning to advance, even though the sea be calm, its roar is heard by those living near the river's mouth, sounding like the tumult of battle heard far off, and soon after the sea with its hissing waves bursts over the bare shoals.

47. Inland from B a r u g a z a the country is inhabited by numerous races — the A r a t r i o i, and the A r a k h o s i o i, and the G a n d a r a i o i, and the people of P r o k l a ï s, in which is B o u k e p h a l o s A l e x a n d r e i a. Beyond these are the B a k t r i a n o i, a most warlike race, governed by their own independent sovereign. It was from these parts Alexander issued to invade India when he marched as far as the Ganges, without, however, attacking Limurikê and the southern parts of the country. Hence up to the present day old *drachmai* bearing the Greek inscriptions of A p o l l o d o t o s and M e n a n d e r are current in Barugaza.

> (47) The account of the 'bore' is followed by an enumeration of the countries around and beyond Barugaza with which it had commercial relations. Inland are the *A r a t r i o i, A r a k h o s i o i, G a n d a r i o i* and the people of *P r o k l a ï s*, a province wherein is Boukephalos Alexandreia, beyond which is the Baktrian nation. It has been thought by some that by the *A r a t r i o i* are meant the Arii, by others that they were the *A r â s t r â s* of Sanskrit called Aratti in the Prakrit, so that the *A r a t r i o i* of the *Periplûs* hold an intermediate place between the Sanskrit and Prakrit form of the name. Müller however says "if you want a people known to the Greeks and Romans as familiarly as the well-known names of the Arakhosii, Gandarii, Peukelitae, you may conjecture that the proper reading is ΔΡΑΝΓΩΝ instead of ΑΡΑΤΡΙΩΝ." It is an error of course on the part of our author when he places *B o u k e p h - a l o s* (a city built by Alexander on the banks of the Hydaspês, where he defeated Pôros), in the neighbourhood of Proklaïs, that is Pekhely in the neighbourhood of Peshawar. He makes a still more surprising error when he states that Alexander penetrated to the Ganges.

48. In the same region eastward is a city called O z ê n ê, formerly the capital wherein the king resided. From it there is brought down to Barugaza every commodity for the supply of the country and for export to our own markets — onyx-stones, porcelain, fine muslins, mallow-coloured muslins, and no small quantity of ordinary cottons. At the same time there is brought down to it from the upper country by way of P r o k l a ï s, for transmission to the coast, Kattybourine,

Patropapigic, and Kabalitic spikenard, and another kind which reaches it by way of the adjacent province of Skythia; also kostus and bdellium.

(48) The next place mentioned in the enumeration is *O z ê n ê* (Ujjain), which, receiving nard through Proklaïs from the distant regions where it was produced, passed it on to the coast for export to the Western World. This aromatic was a product of three districts, whence its varieties were called respectively the *Kattybou-rine*, the *Patropapigic* and the *Kabolitic*. What places were indicated by the first two names cannot be ascertained, but the last points undoubtedly to the region round Kâbul, since its inhabitants are called by Ptolemy *K a b o l i t a i* , and Edrisi uses the term *Myrobal-anos Kabolinos* for the 'myrobolans of Kâbul.' Nard, as Edrisi also observes, has its proper soil in Thibet.

49. The imports of B a r u g a z a are—

Οἶνος προηγουμένος Ἰταλικὸς—Wine, principally Italian.

Καὶ Λαοδικηνὸς καὶ Ἀραβικὸς—Laodikean wine and Arabian.

Χαλκος καὶ κασσίτερος καὶ μόλυβδος—Brass or Copper and Tin and Lead.

Κοράλλιον καὶ χρυσόλιθον—Coral and Gold-stone or Yellow-stone.

Ἱματισμὸς ἁπλοῦς καὶ νόθος πανταῖος—Cloth, plain and mixed, of all sorts.

Πολύμιται ζῶναι πηχυαῖαι—Variegated sashes half a yard wide.

Στύραξ—Storax.

Μελίλωτον—Sweet clover, melilot.

Ὕαλος ἀργὴ—White glass.

Σανδαράκη—Gum Sandarach.

Στίμμι—(Stibium) Tincture for the eyes,—*Sûrmâ*.

Δηνάριον χρυσοῦ καὶ ἀργυροῦν—Gold and Silver specie, yielding a profit when exchanged for native money.

Μύρον οὐ βαρύτιμον οὐδὲ πολὺ—Perfumes or unguents, neither costly nor in great quantity.

In those times, moreover, there were imported, *as presents* to the king, costly silver vases, instruments of music, handsome young women for concubinage, superior wine, apparel, plain but costly, and the choicest unguents. The exports from this part of the country are—

Νὺρδος, κόστος, βδέλλα, ελεφας—Spikenard, costus, bdellium, ivory.

Ὀνυχίνη λιθία καὶ μουρρίνη—Onyx-stones and porcelain.

Λύκιον—*Ruzot*, Box-thorn.

Ὀθόνιον παντοῖον—Cottons of all sorts.

Σηρικὸν—Silk.

Μολόχινον—Mallow-coloured cottons.

Νῆμα—*Silk* thread.

Πέτερι μακρὸν—Long pepper and other articles supplied from the neighbouring ports.

The proper season to set sail for Barugaza from Egypt is the month of July, or Epiphi.

50. From B a r u g a z a the coast immediately adjoining stretches from the north directly to the south, and the country is therefore called D a k h i n a b a d ê s, because Dakhan in the language of the natives signifies *south*. Of this country that part which lies inland towards the east comprises a great space of desert country, and large mountains abounding with all kinds of wild animals, leopards, tigers, elephants, huge snakes, hyenas, and baboons of many different sorts, and is inhabited right across to the Ganges by many and extremely populous nations.

> (50) *B a r u g a z a* had at the same time commercial relations with the Dekhan also. This part of India our author calls *D a k h - i n a b a d ê s*, transliterating the word *D a k s h i n â p a t h a* —(the Dakshinâ, or the South Country). "Here," says Vincent, "the author of the *Periplûs* gives the true direction of this western coast of the Peninsula, and states in direct terms its tendency to the South, while Ptolemy stretches out the whole angle to a straight line, and places the Gulf of Cambay almost in the same latitude as Cape Comorin."

51. Among the marts in this South Country there are two of more particular importance—P a i t h a n a, which lies south from Barugaza, a distance of twenty days, and T a g a r a, ten days east of Paithana, the greatest city in the country. Their commodities are carried down on wagons to Barugaza along roads of extreme difficulty,—that is, from P a i t h a n a a great quantity of onyx-stone, and from T a g a r a ordinary cottons in abundance, many sorts of muslins, mallow-coloured cottons, and other articles of local production brought into it from the parts along the coast. The length of the entire voyage as far as L i m u r i k ê is 700 stadia, and to reach A i g i a l o s you must sail very many stadia further.

> (51) In the interior of the Dekhan, the *Periplûs* places two great seats of commerce, *P a i t h a n a*, 20 days' journey to the south of Barugaza, and *T a g a r a*, 10 days' journey eastward from Paithana. Paithana, which appears in Ptolemy as Baithana, may be identified with *P a i t h a n a. T a g a r a* is more puzzling. Wilford, Vincent, Mannert, Ritter and others identify it with *D ê v a g i r i* or Deogarh, near Elurâ, about 8 miles from Aurangâbâd. The name of a place called Tagarapura occurs in a copper grant of land which was found in the island of Salsette. There is however nothing to show that this was a name of Dêvagiri. Besides, if Paithana be correctly identified, Tagara cannot be Dêvagiri unless the distances and directions are very erroneously given in the *Periplûs*. This is not improbable, and Tagara may therefore be *J u n n a r* (i.e.

Jûna-nagar = *the old city*), which from its position must always have been an emporium, and its Buddha caves belong to about B.C. 100 to A.D. 150 (see *Archæolog. Surv. of West. India*, vol. III., and Elphinstone's *History of India*, p. 223).

Our author introduces us next to another division of India, that called *L i m u r i k ê*, which begins, as he informs us, at a distance of 7,000 stadia (or nearly 900 miles) beyond Barugaza. This estimate is wide of the mark, being in fact about the distance between Barugaza and the southern or remote extremity of Limurikê. In the Indian segment of the Roman maps called from their discoverer, the *Peutinger Tables*, the portion of India to which this name is applied is called *D a m i r i k e*. We can scarcely err, says Dr. Caldwell (*Dravid. Gram.* Intr. page 14), in identifying this name with the Tamil country. If so, the earliest appearance of the name Tamil in any foreign documents will be found also to be most perfectly in accordance with the native Tamil mode of spelling the name. *D a m i r i k e* evidently means *Damirike*.... In another place in the same map a district is called *S c y t i a D y m i r i c e;* and it appears to have been this word which by a mistake of Δ for Λ Ptolemy wrote Λυμιρικὴ. The D retains its place however in the Cosmography of the anonymous geographer of Ravenna, who repeatedly mentions *D i m i r i c a* as one of the three divisions of India and the one furthest to the East. He shows also that the Tamil country must have been meant by the name by mentioning *M o d u r a* as one of the cities it contained.

52. The local marts which occur in order *along the coast* after B a r u g a z a are A k a b a r o u, S o u p p a r a, K a l l i e n a, a city which was raised to the rank of a regular mart in the times of the elder S a r a g a n e s, but after S a n d a n e s became its master its trade was put under the severest restrictions; for if Greek vessels, even by accident, enter its ports, a guard is put on board and they are taken to Barugaza.

(52) Reverting to *B a r u g a z a* our author next enumerates the less important emporia having merely a local trade which intervenes between it and *D i m u r i k ê*. Those are first *A k a b a r o u, S o u p p a r a*, and *K a l l i e n a* —followed by *S e m u l l a, M a n d a g o r a, P a l a i p a t m a i, M e l i g e i z a r a, B u z a n t i o n, T o p e r o n*, and *T u r a n o s b o a s*,—beyond which occurs a succession of islands, some of which give shelter to pirates, and of which the last is called *L e u k ê* or White Island. The actual distance from Barugaza to Naoura, the first port of Dimurikê, is 4,500 stadia.

To take these emporia in detail. *A k a b a r o u* cannot be identified. The reading is probably corrupt. Between the mouths of the Namados and those of the Goaris, Ptolemy interposes Nousaripa, Poulipoula, Ariakê Sadinôn, and Soupara. *N a u s a r i p a* is *N a u s a r i*, about 18 miles to the south of Surat, and *S o u p a r a* is *Sûpârâ* near Vasâï. Benfey, who takes it to be the name of a region and not of a city, regards it as the *Ophir* of the Bible—called in the Septuagint Σωφηρά. *Sôphir*, it may be added, is the Coptic name for India. *Kalliena* is now *Kalyâna* near Bombay [which must have been an important place at an early date. It is named in the Kaṇhêri Bauddha Cave Inscriptions]. It is mentioned by Kosmas (p. 337), who states that it produced copper and sesamum and other kinds of logs, and cloth for wearing apparel. The name *Sandanes*, that of the Prince who sent Greek ships which happened to put into its port under guard to Barugaza, is thought by Benfey to be a territorial title which indicated that he ruled over *Ariakê* of the Sandineis. [But the older "Saraganes" probably indicates one of the great Śâtakarṇi or Ândhrabhṛitya dynasty.] Ptolemy does not mention Kalliena, though he supplies the name of a place omitted in the *Periplûs*, namely *Dounga* (VII. i. 6) near the mouth of the river *Bênda*.

53. After *Kalliena* other local marts occur—*Semulla, Mandagora, Palaipatmai, Melizeigara, Buzantion, Toparon*, and *Turannosboas*. You come next to the islands called *Sêsekreienai* and the island of the *Aigidioi* and that of the *Kaineitai*, near what is called the *Khersonêsos*, places in which are pirates, and after this the island *Leukê* (or 'the White'). Then follow *Naoura* and *Tundis*, the first marts of *Limurikê*, and after these *Mouziris* and *Nelkunda*, the seats of Government.

(53) *Semulla* (in Ptolemy *Timoula* and *Simulla*) is identified by Yule with *Chênval* or Chaul, a seaport 23 miles south of Bombay; [but Bhagvanlâl Indraji suggests Chimûla in Trombay island at the head of the Bombay harbour; and this is curiously supported by one of the Kanhêri inscriptions in which *Chemûla* is mentioned, apparently as a large city, like Supârâ and Kalyâna, in the neighbourhood]. After Simulla Ptolemy mentions *Hippokoura* [possibly, as suggested by the same, a partial translation of *Ghoḍabandar* on the Choḍa nadi in the Ṭhaṅa strait] and *Baltipatna* as places still in Ariakê, but *Mandagara Buzanteion, Khersonêsos, Armagara*, the mouths of the river *Nanagouna*, and an emporium called *Nitra*, as belonging to the Pirate Coast which extended to Dimurikê, of which *Tundis*, he says, is the first city. Ptolemy therefore agrees with our author in assigning the Pirate Coast to the tract of country between Bombay and Goa. This coast continued to be infested with pirates till so late a period as the year 1765, when they were finally exterminated by the British arms. *Mandagara* and *Palaipatma* may have corresponded pretty nearly in situation with the towns of Rájapur and Bankut. Yule places them respectively at Bankut and Debal. *Melizeigara* (Milizêguris or Milizigêris of Ptolemy, VII. i. 95), Vincent identifies with Jaygaḍh or Sidê Jay-

gaḍh. The same place appears in Pliny as *S i g e r u s* (VI. xxvi. 100). Buzantium may be referred to about Vijayadrug or Esvantgadh, *T o p a r o n* may be a corrupt reading for *T o g a r o n*, and may perhaps therefore be Devagaḍh which lies a little beyond Vijayndrug. *T u r a n n o s b o a s* is not mentioned elsewhere, but it may have been, us Yule suggests, the Bandâ or Tirakal river. Müller placed it at Acharê. The first island on this part of the coast is Sindhudrug near Mâlwan, to which succeeds a group called the Burnt Islands, among which the Vingorla rocks are conspicuous. These are no doubt the *H e p t a n ê s i a* of Ptolemy (VII. i. 95), and probably the *S ê s i k r i e n a i* of the *Periplûs*. The island Aigidion called that of the Aigidii may be placed at Goa, [but Yule suggests Angediva south of Sadaśivagaḍh, in lat. 14° 45′ N., which is better]. Kaineiton may be the island of St. George.

We come next to *N a o u r a* in Dimurikê. This is now *H o n â - v a r*, written otherwise Onore, situated on the estuary of a broad river, the *S a r â v a t î*, on which are the falls of Gêrsappa, one of the most magnificent and stupendous cataracts in the world. If the *N i t r a* of Ptolemy (VII. i. 7) and the *N i t r i a* of Pliny be the same as *N a o u r a*, then these authors extend the pirate coast a little further south than the *Periplûs* does. But if they do not, and therefore agree in their views as to where Dimurikê begins, the *N i t r a* may be placed, Müller thinks, at Mirjan or Komta, which is not far north from Honâvar. [Yule places it at Mangalur.] Müller regards the first supposition however as the more probable, and quotes at length a passage from Pliny (VI. xxvi. 104) referring thereto, which must have been excerpted from some *Periplûs* like our author's, but not from it as some have thought. "To those bound for India it is most convenient to depart from Okêlis. They sail thence with the wind Hipalus in 40 days to the first emporium of India, Muziris, which is not a desirable place to arrive at on account of pirates infesting the neighbourhood, who hold a place called *N i t r i a s*, while it is not well supplied with merchandize. Besides, the station for ships is at a great distance from the shore, and cargoes have both to be landed and to be shipped by means of little boats. There reigned there when I wrote this *C a e l o b o - t h r a s*. Another port belonging to the nation is more convenient, *N e a c y n d o n*, which is called *B e c a r e* (*sic. codd.*, Barace, Harduin and Sillig). There reigned Pandiôn in an inland town far distant from the emporium called *M o d u r a*. The region, however, from which they convey pepper to Becare in boats formed from single logs is *C o t t o n a r a*."

54. To the kingdom under the sway of K ê p r o b o t r e s [22] Tundis is subject, a village of great note situate near the sea. M o u z i r i s, which pertains to the

---

[22] *Ind. Ant.* vol. I. pp. 309-310.

same realm, is a city at the height of prosperity, frequented as it is by ships from A r i a k ê and Greek ships *from Egypt*. It lies near a river at a distance from Tundis of 500 stadia, whether this is measured from river to river or by the length of the sea voyage, and it is 20 stadia distant from the mouth of its own river. The distance of N e l k u n d a from M o u z i r i s also nearly 500 stadia, whether measured from river to river or by the sea voyage, but it belongs to a different kingdom, that of P a n d i ô n . It likewise is situate near a river and at about a distance from the sea of 120 stadia.

(54) With regard to the names in this extract which occur also in the *Periplûs* the following passages quoted from Dr. Caldwell's *Dravidian Grammar* will throw much light. He says (Introd. p. 97):—"M u z i r i s appears to be the *M u y i r i* of Muyiri-kotta. Tyndis is *T u ṇ ḍ i*, and the Kynda, of Nelkynda, or as Ptolemy has it, Melkynda, *i. e.* probably Western kingdom, seems to be *K a n n e t t r i*, the southern boundary of Kêrala proper. One MS. of Pliny writes the second part of this word not *Cyndon* but *Canidon*. The first of these places was identified by Dr. Gundert, for the remaining two we are indebted to Dr. Burnell.

"Cottonara, Pliny; Kottonarike, *Periplûs*, the district where the best pepper was produced. It is singular that this district was not mentioned by Ptolemy. *C o t t o n a r a* was evidently the name of the district. κοττοναρικον the name of the pepper for which the district was famous. Dr. Buchanan identifies Cottonara with *K a ḍ a t t a - n a ḍ u*, the name of a district in the Calicut country celebrated for its pepper. Dr. Burnell identifies it with *K o ḷ a t t a - n â ḍ u*, the district about Tellicherry which he says is the pepper district. *Kadatta* in Malayâlam means 'transport, conveyance,' *N â d û*, Tam.—Mal., means a district."

"The prince called Kêrobothros by Ptolemy (VII. i. 86) is called Kêprobotros by the author of the *Periplûs*. The insertion of π is clearly an error, but more likely to be the error of a copyist than that of the author, who himself had visited the territories of the prince in question. He is called Caelobothras in Pliny's text, but one of the MSS. gives it more correctly as Celobotras. The name in Sanskrit, and in full is 'Keralaputra,' but both *kêra* and *kêla* are Dravidian abbreviations of *kêralâ*. They are Malayâlam however, not Tamil abbreviations, and the district over which Keralaputra ruled is that in which the Malayâlam language is now spoken" (p. 95). From Ptolemy we learn that the capital of this prince was *K a r o u r a*, which has been "identified with *K a r û r*, an important town in the Koimbatur district originally included in the Chêra kingdom. Karûr means the black town.... Ptolemy's word *K a r o u r a* represents the Tamiḷ name of the place with perfect accuracy." Nelkunda, our author informs us, was not subject to this prince but to another called *P a n d i ô n* . This name, says Dr. Caldwell, "is of Sanskrit origin, and *Pandæ*, the form which Pliny, after Megasthenês, gives in his list of the Indian nations, comes very near the Sanskrit. The more recent local information of Pliny himself, as well as the notices of Ptolemy and the *Periplûs*, supply us with the Dravidian form of the word. The Tamil̤ sign of the masc. sing. is *an*, and Tamil̤ inserts *i* euphonically after *ṇḍ*, consequently Pandiôn, and still better the plural form of the word *Pandiones*, faithfully represents the Tamil̤ masc. sing. *Pâṇḍiyan*." In another passage the same scholar says: "The Sanskrit Pâṇḍya is written in Tamil Pâṇḍiya, but the more completely tamilized form *Pâṇḍi* is still more commonly used all over southern India. I derive Pâṇḍi, as native scholars always derive the word, from the Sanskrit Pâṇḍu, the name of the father of the Pâṇḍava brothers." The capital of this prince, as Pliny has stated, was *Modura*, which is the Sanskrit Maṭhurâ pronounced in the Tamil̤ manner. The corresponding city in Northern India, Maṭhurâ, is written by the Greeks *Methora*.

Nelkunda is mentioned by various authors under varying forms of the name. As has been already stated, it is Melkunda in Ptolemy, who places it in the country of the Aii. In the *Peutingerian Table* it is Nincylda, and in the Geographer of Ravenna, Nilcinna. At the mouth of the river on which it stands was its shipping port *Bakare* or Becare, according to Müller now represented by *Markari* (lat. 12° N.) Yule conjectures that it must have been between Kanetti and Kolum in Travancore. Regarding the trade of this place we may quote a remark from Vincent. "We find," he says, "that throughout the whole which the *Periplûs* mentions of India we have a catalogue of the exports and imports only at the two ports of Barugaza and Nelcynda, and there seems to be a distinction fixed between the articles appropriate to each. Fine muslins and ordinary cottons are the principal commodities of the first; tortoise shell, precious stones, silk, and above all pepper, seem to have been procurable only at the latter. This pepper is said to be brought to this port from Cottonara, famous to this hour for producing the best pepper in the world except that of Sumatra. The pre-eminence of these two ports will account for the little that is said of the others by the author, and why he has left us so few characters by which we may distinguish one from another."

Our author on concluding his account of Nelkunda interrupts his narrative to relate the incidents of the important discovery of the monsoon made by that Columbus of antiquity Hippalus. This account, Vincent remarks, naturally excites a curiosity in the mind to enquire how it should happen that the monsoon should have been noticed by Nearkhos, and that from the time of his voyage for 300 years no one should have attempted a direct course till

Hippalus ventured to commit himself to the ocean. He is of opinion that there was a direct passage by the monsoons both in going to and coming from India in use among the Arabians before the Greeks adopted it, and that Hippalus frequenting these seas as a pilot or merchant, had met with Indian or Arabian traders who made their voyages in a more compendious manner than the Greeks, and that he collected information from them which he had both the prudence and courage to adopt, just as Columbus, while owing much to his own nautical experience and fortitude was still under obligations to the Portuguese, who had been resolving the great problems in the art of navigation for almost a century previous to his expedition.

55. At the very mouth of this river lies another village, B a k a r e , to which the ships despatched from Nelkunda come down *empty* and ride at anchor off shore while taking in cargo: for the river, it may be noted, has sunken reefs and shallows which make its navigation difficult. The sign by which those who come hither by sea know they are nearing land is their meeting with snakes, which are here of a black colour, not so long as those already mentioned, like serpents about the head, and with eyes the colour of blood.

(55) *N e l k u n d a* appears to have been the limit of our author's voyage along the coast of India, for in the sequel of his narrative he defines but vaguely the situation of the places which he notices, while his details are scanty, and sometimes grossly inaccurate. Thus he makes the Malabar Coast extend southwards beyond Cape Comorin as far at least as Kolkhoi (near Tutikorin) on the Coromandel coast, and like many ancient writers, represents Ceylon as stretching westward almost as far as Africa.

56. The ships which frequent these ports are of a large size, on account of the great amount and bulkiness of the pepper and betel of which their lading consists. The imports here are principally—

Χρήματα πλεῖστα—Great quantities of specie.

Χρυσόλιθα—(Topaz?) Gold-stone, Chrysolite.

Ἱματισμὸς ἁπλοὸς οὐ πολὺς—A small assortment of plain cloth.

Πολύμιτα—Flowered robes.

Στίμμι, κοράλλιον—Stibium, a pigment for the eyes, coral.

ὕαλος ἀργὴ χαλκὸς—White glass, copper or brass.

Κασσίτερος, μόλυβδος—Tin, lead.

Οἶνος οὐ πολύς, ὡσεὶ δὲ τοσοῦτον ὅσον ἐν Βαρυγάζοις—Wine but not much, but about as much as at Barugaza.

Σανδαράκη—Sandarach (*Sindûrâ*).

Ἀρσενικὸν—Arsenic (Orpiment), yellow sulphuret of arsenic.

Σῖτος ὅσος ἀρκέ σει τοῖς περὶ το ναυκλήριον, διὰ τὸ μὴ τοὺς ἐμπόρους αὐτῷ χρῆσθαι—Corn, only for the use of the ship's company, as the merchants do not sell it.

The following commodities are brought to it for export:—

Πέπερι μονογενῶς ἐν ἐνὶ τόπω τούτων τῶν ἐμπορίων γεννώμενον πολύ τῇ λεγομενῇ Κοττοναρικη—Pepper in great quantity, produced in only one of these marts, and called the pepper of Kottonara.

Μαργαρίτης ἱκανὸς καὶ διάφορος—Pearls in great quantity and of superior quality.

Ἐλέφας—Ivory.

Ὀθόνια Σηρικὰ—Fine silks.

Νάρδος ἡ Γαγγητικὴ—Spikenard from the Ganges.

Μαλάβαθρον—Betel—all brought from countries further east.

Λιθία διαφανὴς παντοία—Transparent or precious stones of all sorts.

Ἀδάμας—Diamonds.

Ὑάκινθος—Jacinths.

Χελώνη ἥτε Χρυσονησιωτικὴ καὶ ἡ περὶ τὰς νήσους θηρευομένη τὰς προκειμένας αὐτῆς τῆς Λιμυρικῆς—Tortoise-shell from the Golden Island, and another sort which is taken in the islands which lie off the coast of Limurikê.

The proper season to set sail from Egypt for this part of India is about the month of July—that is, Epiphi.

57. The whole round of the voyage from K a n ê and E u d a i m ô n A r a b i a , which we have just described, used to be performed in small vessels which kept close to shore and followed its windings, but H i p p a l o s was the pilot who first, by observing the bearings of the ports and the configuration of the sea, discovered the direct course across the ocean; whence as, at the season when our own Etesians are blowing, a periodical wind from the ocean likewise blows in the Indian Sea, this wind, which is the south-west, is, it seems, called in these seas Hippalos [after the name of the pilot who first discovered the *passage by means of it*]. From the time of this discovery to the present day, merchants who sail for India either from K a n ê, or, as others do, from A r ô m a t a , if Limurikê be their destination, must often change their tack, but if they are bound for B a r u g a z a and S k y - t h i a , they are not retarded for more than three days, after which, committing themselves to the monsoon which blows right in the direction of their course, they stand far out to sea, leaving all the gulfs we have mentioned in the distance.

58. After B a k a r e occurs the mountain called Pyrrhos (or the Red) towards the south, near another district of the country called P a r a l i a (where the pearl-fisheries are which belong to king Pandiôn), and a city of the name of K o l k h o i . In this tract the first place met with is called B a l i t a , which has a good harbour and a village on its shore. Next to this is another place called K o m a r , where is the cape of the same name and a haven. Those who wish to consecrate the closing part

of their lives to religion come hither and bathe and engage themselves to celibacy. This is also done by women; since it is related that the goddess (*Kumârî*) once on a time resided at the place and bathed. From K o m a r e i (towards the south) the country extends as far as K o l k h o i , where the fishing for pearls is carried on. Condemned criminals are employed in this service. King Pandiôn is the owner of the fishery. To K o l k h o i succeeds another coast lying along a gulf having a district in the interior bearing the name of A r g a l o u . In this single place are obtained the pearls collected near the island of E p i o d ô r o s . From it are exported the muslins called *ebargareitides*.

> (58) The first place mentioned after *B a k a r e* is *P y r r h o s ,* or the Red Mountain, which extends along a district called *P a r a - l i a* . "There are," says Dr. Caldwell (Introd. p. 99), "three Paralias mentioned by the Greeks, two by Ptolemy ... one by the author of the *Periplûs*. The Paralia mentioned by the latter corresponded to Ptolemy's country of the Ἄϊοι, and that of the Καρεοι, that is, to South Travancore and South Tinnevelly. It commenced at the Red Cliffs south of Quilon, and included not only Cape Comorin but also Κόλχοι, where the pearl fishing was carried on, which belonged to King Pandiôn. Dr. Burnell identifies Paralia with Parali, which he states is an old name for Travancore, but I am not quite able to adopt this view." "Paralia," he adds afterwards, "may possibly have corresponded in meaning, if not in sound, to some native word meaning coast, — viz., Karei." On this coast is a place called *B a l i t a* , which is perhaps the *B a m m a l a* of Ptolemy (VII. i. 9), which Mannert identifies with Manpalli, a little north of Anjenga.

60. Among the marts and anchorages along this shore to which merchants from Limurikê and the north resort, the most conspicuous are K a m a r a and P o d o u k ê and S ô p a t m a , which occur in the order in which we have named them. In these marts are found those native vessels for coasting voyages which trade as far as Limurikê, and another kind called *sangara*, mode by fastening together large vessels formed each of a single timber, and also others called *kolandiophônta*, which are of great bulk and employed for voyages to K h r u s ê and the G a n g e s . These marts import all the commodities which reach Limurikê for commercial purposes, absorbing likewise nearly every species of goods brought from Egypt, and most descriptions of all the goods exported from Limurikê and disposed of on this coast *of India.*

> (60) We now reach the great promontory called in the *Periplûs K o m a r* and *K o m a r e i* , Cape Kumârî. "It has derived its name," says Caldwell, "from the Sans. *Kumârî*, a virgin, one of the names of the goddess Durgâ, the presiding divinity of the place, but the shape which this word has taken is, especially in *komar*, distinctively Tamilian." In ordinary Tamil *Kumârî* becomes *Kumări*; and in the vulgar dialect of the people residing in the neighbourhood of the Cape a virgin is neither Kumârî nor Kumări but Kŭmăr

pronounced Kŏmar. It is remarkable that this vulgar corruption of the Sanskrit is identical with the name given to the place by the author of the *Periplûs*.... The monthly bathing in honor of the goddess Durgâ is still continued at Cape Comorin, but is not practised to the same extent as in ancient times.... Through the continued encroachments of the sea, the harbour the Greek mariners found at Cape Comorin and the fort (if φρουριον is the correct reading for βριάριον of the MS.) have completely disappeared; but a fresh water well remains in the centre of a rock, a little way out at sea. Regarding *K o l k h o i*, the next place mentioned after Komari, the same authority as we have seen places it (*Ind. Ant.* vol. VI. p. 80) near Tuticorin. It is mentioned by Ptolemy and in the *Peutinger Tables*, where it is called 'Colcis Indorum'. The Gulf of Manaar was called by the Greeks the Colchic Gulf. The Tamiḷ name of the place Kolkei is almost identical with the Greek. "The place," according to Caldwell, "is now about three miles inland, but there are abundant traces of its having once stood on the coast, and I have found the tradition that it was once the seat of the pearl fishery, still surviving amongst its inhabitants." After the sea had retired from Κόλχοι ... a new emporium arose on the coast. This was *K â y a l*, the Cael of Marco Polo. Kâyal in turn became in time too far from the sea ... and Tuticorin (*T û t t r u k u ḍ i*) was raised instead by the Portuguese from the position of a fishing village to that of the most important port on the southern Coromandel coast. The identification of Kolkoi with Kolkei is one of much importance. Being perfectly certain it helps forward other identifications. *Kol.* in Tamiḷ means 'to slay.' *Kei* is 'hand.' It was the first capital of Pandiôn.

The coast beyond *K o l k h o i*, which has an inland district belonging to it called *A r g a l o u*, is indented by a gulf called by Ptolemy the Argarik—now Palk Bay. Ptolemy mentions also a promontory called *K ô r u* and beyond it a city called *A r g e i r o u* and an emporium called *S a l o u r*. This Kôru of Ptolemy, Caldwell thinks, represents the *K ô l i s* of the geographers who preceded him, and the *K o ṭ i* of Tamiḷ, and identifies it with "the island promontory of *R â m e ś v a r a m*, the point of land from which there was always the nearest access from Southern India to Ceylon." An island occurs in these parts, called that of *E p i o d ô r o s*, noted for its pearl fishery, on which account Ritter would identify it with the island of Manaar, which Ptolemy, as Mannert thinks, speaks of as Νάνιγηρίς (VII. i. 95). Müller thinks, however, it may be compared with Ptolemy's *K ô r u*, and so be Râmeśvaram.

This coast has commercial intercourse not only with the Malabar ports, but also with the Ganges and the Golden Khersonese. For the trade with the former a species of canoes was used called *Sangara*. The Malayâlam name of these, Caldwell says, is *Changâdam*, in Tuḷa *Jangâla*, compare Sanskrit *Samghâdam* a raft (*Ind. Ant.* vol. I. p. 309). The large vessels employed for the Eastern trade were called *Kolandiophonta*, a name which Caldwell confesses his inability to explain.

Three cities and ports are named in the order of their occurrence which were of great commercial importance, *K a m a r a*, *P o d o u k ê*, and *S ô p a t m a*. *K a m a r a* may perhaps be, as Müller thinks, the emporium which Ptolemy calls *K h a b ê r i s*, situated at the mouth of the River *K h a b ê r o s* (now, the Kavery), perhaps, as Dr. Burnell suggests, the modern Kaveripattam. (*Ind. Ant.* vol. VII. p. 40). *P o d o u k ê* appears in Ptolemy as Podoukê. It is *P u d u c h c h ê r i*, *i. e.* 'new town,' now well known as Pondicherry; so Bohlen, Ritter, and Benfey. [Yule and Lassen place it at Pulikât]. *S ô p a t m a* is not mentioned in Ptolemy, nor can it now be traced. In Sanskrit it transliterates into *Su-patna*, *i. e.*, fair town.

61. Near the region which succeeds, where the course of the voyage now bends to the east, there lies out in the open sea stretching towards the west the island now called P a l a i s i m o u n d o u, but by the ancients T a p r o b a n ê. To cross over to the northern side of it takes a day. In the south part it gradually stretches towards the west till it nearly reaches the opposite coast of A z a n i a. It produces pearl, precious (*transparent*) stones, muslins, and tortoise-shell.

(61) The next place noticed is the Island of Ceylon, which is designated *P a l a i s i m o u n d o u*, with the remark that its former name was *T a p r o b a n ê*. This is the Greek transliteration of Tâmraparnî, the name given by a band of colonists from Magadha to the place where they first landed in Ceylon, and which was afterwards extended to the whole island. It is singular, Dr. Caldwell remarks, that this is also the name of the principal river in Tinnevelly on the opposite coast of India, and he infers that the colony referred to might previously have formed a settlement in Tinnevelly at the mouth of the Tâmraparṇi river—perhaps at Kolkei, the earliest residence of the Pâṇḍya kings. The passage in the *Periplûs* which refers to the island is very corrupt.

62.(*Returning to the coast,*) not far from the three marts we have mentioned lies M a s a l i a, the seaboard of a country extending far inland. Here immense quantities of fine muslins are manufactured. From M a s a l i a the course of the voyage lies eastward across a neighbouring bay to D ê s a r ê n ê, which has the breed of elephants called Bôsarê. Leaving D ê s a r ê n ê the course is northerly, passing a variety of barbarous tribes, among which are the K i r r h a d a i, savages whose noses are flattened to the face, and another tribe, that of the B a r g u s o i, as well as the H î p p i o p r o s ô p o i *or* M a k r o p r o s ô p o i (the horse faced or long faced men), who are reported to be cannibals.

(62) Recurring to the mainland, the narrative notices a district

called *M a s a l i a*, where great quantities of cotton were manufactured. This is the *M a ï s ô l i a* of Ptolemy, the region in which he
places the mouths of a river the *M a i s ô l o s*, which Benfey identifies with the Godâvarî, in opposition to others who would make
it the Krishnâ, which is perhaps Ptolemy's *T u n a*. The name
Maisôlia is taken from the Sanskrit Mausala, preserved in Machh-
lipatana, now Masulipatam. Beyond this, after an intervening gulf
running eastward is crossed, another district occurs, *D e s a r ê n ê*,
noted for its elephants. This is not mentioned by Ptolemy, but a
river with a similar name, the *D ô s a r ô n*, is found in his enumeration of the rivers which occur between the Maisôlos and the
Ganges. As it is the last in the list it may probably be, as Lassen
supposes, the Brâhmini. Our author however places Desarênê at a
much greater distance from the Ganges, for he peoples the intermediate space with a variety of tribes which Ptolemy relegates to
the East of the river. The first of these tribes is that of the *K i r r â -
d a i* (Sanskrit, Kirâtas), whose features are of the Mongolian type.
Next are the *B a r g u s o i*, not mentioned by Ptolemy, but perhaps
to be identified with the cannibal race he speaks of, the *B a r o u s -
a i* thought by Yule to be possibly the inhabitants of the Nikobar
islands, and lastly the tribe of the long or horse-faced men who
were also cannibals.

63. After passing these the course turns again to the east, and if you sail with
the ocean to your right and the coast far to your left, you reach the Ganges and
the extremity of the continent towards the east *called* K h r u s ê (the Golden Khersonese). The river of this region called the G a n g e s is the largest in India; it has
an *annual* increase and decrease like the Nile, and there is on it a mart called after
it, Gangê, through which passes *a considerable traffic* consisting of betel, the Gangetic spikenard, pearl, and the finest of all muslins—those called the Gangetic. In
this locality also there is said to be a gold mine and a gold coin called *Kaltis*. Near
this river there is an island of the ocean called K h r u s ê (or the Golden), which
lies directly under the rising sun and at the extremity of the world towards the
east. It produces the finest tortoise-shell that is found throughout the whole of the
Erythræan Sea.

(63) When this coast of savages and monsters is left behind,
the course lies eastward, and leads to the Ganges, which is the
greatest river of India, and adjoins the extremity of the Eastern
continent called *K h r u s ê*, or the Golden. Near the river, or, according to Ptolemy, on the third of its mouths stands a great
emporium of trade called *G a n g ê*, exporting *Malabathrum* and
cottons and other commodities. Its exact position there are not
sufficient data to determine. Khrusê is not only the name of the
last part of the continent, but also of an island lying out in the
ocean to eastward, not far from the Ganges. It is the last part of
the world which is said to be inhabited. The situation of Khrusê is

differently defined by different ancient authors. It was not known to the Alexandrine geographers. Pliny seems to have preserved the most ancient report circulated regarding it. He says (VI. xxiii. 80): "Beyond the mouth of the Indus are *C h r y s e* and *A r g y r e* abounding in metals as I believe, for I can hardly credit what some have related that the soil consists of gold and silver." Mela (III. 7) assigns to it a very different position, asserting it to be near *T a b i s*, the last spur of the range of Taurus. He therefore places it where Eratosthenês places *T h î n a i*, to the north of the Ganges on the confines of the Indian and Skythian oceans. Ptolemy, in whose time the Transgangetic world was better known, refers it to the peninsula of Malacca, the Golden Khersonese.

64. Beyond this region, immediately under the north, where the sea terminates outwards, there lies somewhere in T h î n a a very great city,—not on the coast, but in the interior of the country, called T h î n a ,—from which silk, whether in the raw state or spun into thread and woven into cloth, is brought by land to Barugaza through Baktria, or by the Ganges to Limurikê. To penetrate into T h î n a is not an easy undertaking, and but few *merchants* come from it, and that rarely. Its situation is under the Lesser Bear, and it is said to be conterminous with the remotest end of Pontos, and that part of the Kaspian Sea which adjoins the Maiôtic Lake, along with which it issues by *one and* the same mouth into the ocean.

(64) The last place which the *Periplûs* mentions is Thînai, an inland city of the *T h î n a i* or *S i n a i*, having a large commerce in silk and woollen stuffs. The ancient writers are not at all agreed as to its position. Colonel Yule thinks it was probably the city described by Marco Polo under the name of *K e n j a n - f u* (that is Singan-fu or Chauggan,) the most celebrated city in Chinese history, and the capital of several of the most potent dynasties. It was the metropolis of Shi Hwengti of the T'Sin dynasty, properly the first emperor, and whose conquests almost intersected those of his contemporary Ptolemy Euergetês—(vide Yule's *Travels of Marco Polo*, vol. II. p. 21).

65. On the confines, however, of T h î n a i an annual fair is held, attended by a race of men of squat figure, with their face very broad, but mild in disposition, called the S e s a t a i , who in appearance resemble wild animals. They come with their wives and children to this fair, bringing heavy loads of goods wrapped up in mats resembling in outward appearance the early leaves of the vine. Their place of assembly is where their own territory borders with that of Thînai; and here, squatted on the mats on which they exhibit their wares, they feast for several days, after which they return to their homes in the interior. On observing their retreat the people of Thînai, repairing to the spot, collect the mats on which they had been sitting, and taking out the fibres, which are called *petroi*, from the reeds, they put the leaves two and two together, and roll them up into slender balls, through which they pass the fibres extracted from the reeds. Three kinds of Malabathrum are thus made—that of the large ball, that of the middle, and that of the small, ac-

cording to the size of the leaf of which the balls are formed. Hence there are three kinds of Malabathrum, which after being made up are forwarded to India by the manufacturers.

66. All the regions beyond this are unexplored, being difficult of access by reason of the extreme rigour of the climate and the severe frosts, or perhaps because such is the will of the divine power.

THE VOYAGE OF NEARKHOS,

FROM THE INDUS TO THE HEAD OF THE PERSIAN GULF,

AS DESCRIBED IN THE SECOND PART OF THE INDIKA OF ARRIAN,

(FROM CHAPTER XVIII. TO THE END.)

TRANSLATED FROM MÜLLER'S EDITION

(As given in the *Geographi Græci Minores*: Paris, 1855).

WITH INTRODUCTION AND NOTES.

THE VOYAGE OF NEARKHOS.

INTRODUCTION.

The coasting voyage from the mouth of the Indus to the head of the Persian Gulf, designed by Alexander the Great, and executed by Nearkhos, may be regarded as the most important achievement of the ancients in navigation. It opened up, as Vincent remarks, a communication between Europe and the most distant countries of Asia, and, at a later period, was the source and origin of the Portuguese discoveries, and consequently the primary cause, however remote, of the British establishments in India. A Journal of this voyage was written by Nearkhos himself, which, though not extant in its original form, has been preserved for us by Arrian, who embodied its contents in his little work on India,[23] which he wrote as a sequel to his history of the expedition of Alexander.

Nearkhos as a writer must be acknowledged to be most scrupulously honest and exact,—for the result of explorations made in modern times along the shores which he passed in the course of his voyage shows that his description of them is accurate even in the most minute particulars. His veracity was nevertheless oppugned in ancient times by Strabo, who unjustly stigmatises the whole class of the Greek writers upon India as mendacious. "Generally speaking," he says (II. i. 9), "the men who have written upon Indian affairs were a set of liars. Deimakhos holds the first place in the list, Megasthenês comes next, while Onêsikritos and Nearkhos, with others of the same class, stammer out a few words of truth." ($\pi\alpha\varrho\alpha\psi\epsilon\lambda\lambda\acute{\iota}\zeta o\nu\tau\epsilon\varsigma$). Strabo, however, in spite of this censure did not hesitate to use Nearkhos as one of his chief authorities for his description of India, and is indebted to him for many facts relating to that country, which, however extraordinary they might appear to his contemporaries, have been all confirmed by subsequent observation. It is therefore fairly open to doubt whether Strabo was altogether sincere in his ill opinion, seeing it had but little, if any, influence on his practice. We know at all events that he was too much inclined to undervalue any writer who retailed fables, without discriminating whether the writer set them down as facts, or merely as stories, which he had gathered from hearsay.

In modern times, the charge of mendacity has been repeated by Hardouin and Huet. There are, however, no more than two passages of the Journal which can be adduced to support this imputation. The first is that in which the excessive breadth of 200 stadia is given to the Indus, and the second that in which it is asserted that at Malana (situated in 25° 17′ of N. latitude) the shadows at noon were observed to fall southward, and this in the month of November. With regard to the first charge, it may be supposed that the breadth assigned to the Indus was probably that which it was observed to have when in a state of inundation, and with

[23] Written in the Ionic dialect.

regard to the second, it may be met by the supposition, which is quite admissible, that Arrian may have misapprehended in some measure the import of the statement as made by Nearkhos. The passage will be afterwards examined,[24] but in the meantime we may say, with Vincent, that if the difficulty it presents admits of no satisfactory solution, the misstatement ought not, as standing alone, to be insisted upon to the invalidation of the whole work.

But another charge besides that of mendacity has been preferred against the Journal. Dodwell has denied its authenticity. His attack is based on the following passage in Pliny (VI. 23):—Onesciriti et Nearchi navigatio nec nomina habet mansionum nec spatia. *The Journal of Onesicritus and Nearchus has neither the names of the anchorages nor the measure of the distances.* From this Dodwell argues that, as the account of the voyage in Arrian contains both the names and the distances, it could not have been a transcript of the Journal of Nearkhos, which according to Pliny gave neither names nor distances. Now, in the first place, it may well be asked, why the authority of Pliny, who is by no means always a careful writer, should be set so high as to override all other testimony, for instance, that of Arrian himself, who expressly states in the outset of his narrative that he intended to give the account of the voyage which had been written by Nearkhos. In the second place, the passage in question is probably corrupt, or if not, it is in direct conflict with the passage which immediately follows it, and contains Pliny's own summary of the voyage in which little else is given than the names of the anchorages and the distances. Dodwell was aware of the inconsistency of the two passages, and endeavoured to explain it away. In this he entirely fails, and there can therefore be no reasonable doubt, that in Arrian's work we have a record of the voyage as authentic as it is veracious.

Of that record we proceed to give a brief abstract, adding a few particulars gathered from other sources.

The fleet with which Nearkhos accomplished the voyage consisted of war-galleys and transports which had been partly built and partly collected on the banks of the river Hydaspes (now the Jhelam), where Alexander had supplied them with crews by selecting from his troops such men as had a knowledge of seamanship. The fleet thus manned sailed slowly down the Hydaspes, the Akesinês, and the Indus, its movements being regulated by those of the army, which, in marching down towards the sea, was engaged in reducing the warlike tribes settled along the banks of these rivers. This downward voyage occupied, according to Strabo, ten months, but it probably did not occupy more than nine. The fleet having at length reached the apex of the Delta formed by the Indus remained in that neighbourhood for some time at a place called Pattala, which has generally been identified with Ṭhaṭha—a town near to where the western arm of the Indus bifurcates,—but which Cunningham and others would prefer to identify with Nirankol or Haidarâbâd.[25] From Pattala Alexander sailed down the western stream of the river, where some of his ships were damaged and others destroyed by encountering the

---

[24] See infra, note 35.
[25] Geog. of Anc. India, p. 279 sqq.

Bore, a phenomenon as alarming as it was new to the Greeks.[26] He returned to Pattala, and thence made an excursion down the Eastern stream, which he found less difficult to navigate. On again returning to Pattala he removed his fleet down to a station on the Western branch of the river (at an island called Killouta),[27] which was at no great distance from the sea. He then set out on his return to Persia, leaving instructions with Nearkhos to start on the voyage as soon as the calming of the monsoon should render navigation safe. It was the king's intention to march near to the coast, and to collect at convenient stations supplies for the victualling of the fleet, but he found that such a route was impracticable, and he was obliged to lead his army through the inland provinces which lay between India and his destination, Sûsa.[28] He left Leonnatos, however, behind him in the country of the Oreitai, with instructions to render every assistance in his power to the expedition under Nearkhos when it should reach that part of the coast.

Nearkhos remained in the harbour at Killouta for about a month after Alexander had departed, and then sailed during a temporary lull in the monsoon, as he was apprehensive of being attacked by the natives who had been but imperfectly subjugated, and whose spirit was hostile.[29] The date on which he set sail is fixed by Vincent as the 1st of October in the year B.C. 326. He proceeded slowly down the river, and anchored first at a place called Stoura, which was only 100 stadia distant from the station they had quitted. Here the fleet remained for two days, when it proceeded to an anchorage only 30 stadia farther down the stream at a place called Kaumana.[30] Thence it proceeded to Koreatis (v. 1. Koreëstis)—where it again anchored. When once more under weigh its progress was soon arrested by a dangerous rock or bar which obstructed the mouth of the river.[31] After some delay this difficulty was overcome, and the fleet was conducted in safety into the open main, and onward to an island called Krôkala (150 stadia distant from the bar), where it remained at anchor throughout the day following its arrival. On leaving this island Nearkhos had Mount Eiros (now Manora) on his right hand, and a low flat island on his left; and this, as Cunningham remarks, is a very accurate description of the entrance to Karâchi harbour. The fleet was conducted into this harbour, now so well known as the great emporium of the trade of the Indus, and here, as the monsoon was still blowing with great violence, it remained for four and twenty days. The harbour was so commodious and secure that Nearkhos designated it the Port of Alexander. It was well sheltered by an island lying close to its mouth, called by Arrian, Bibakta, but by Pliny, Bibaga, and by Philostratos, Biblos.

The expedition took its departure from this station on the 3rd of November. It suffered both from stress of weather and from shortness of provisions until it

[26] See Arrian's Anab. VI. 19. Καὶ τοῦτο οὔπω πρότερον εγνωκόσι τοῖς ἀμφ' Ἀλέξανδρον ἔκπληξιν μὲν καὶ αὐτὸ οὐ σμικρὰν παρέσχε.

[27] See Arrian, ib.

[28] See id. VI. 23, and Strab. xv. ii. 3, 4.

[29] Strab. ib. 5.

[30] This may perhaps be represented by the modern Khâu, the name of one of the western mouths of the Indus.

[31] See infra, p. 176, note 17.

reached Kôkala on the coast of the Oreitai, where it took on board the supplies which had been collected for its use by the exertions of Leonnatos. Here it remained for about 10 days, and by the time of its departure the monsoon had settled in its favour, so that the courses daily accomplished were now of much greater length than formerly. The shores, however, of the Ikhthyophagoi, which succeeded to those of the Oreitai, were so miserably barren and inhospitable that provisions were scarcely procurable, and Nearkhos was apprehensive lest the men, famished and despairing, should desert the ships. Their sufferings were not relieved till they approached the straits, which open into the Persian Gulf. When within the straits, they entered the mouth of the river Anamis (now the Minâb or Ibrahim river), and having landed, formed a dockyard and a camp upon its banks. This place lay in Harmozeia, a most fertile and beautiful district belonging to Karmania. Nearkhos, having here learned that Alexander was not more than a 5 days' journey from the sea, proceeded into the interior to meet him, and report the safety of the expedition. During his absence the ships were repaired and provisioned, and therefore soon after his return to the camp he gave orders for the resumption of the voyage. The time spent at Harmozeia was one and twenty days. The fleet again under weigh coasted the islands lying at the mouth of the gulf, and then having shaped its course towards the mainland, passed the western shores of Karmania and those of Persis, till it arrived at the mouth of the Sitakos (now the Kara-Agach), where it was again repaired and supplied with provisions, remaining for the same number of days as at the Anamis. One of the next stations at which it touched was Mesembria, which appears to have been situated in the neighbourhood of the modern Bushire. The coast of Persis was difficult to navigate on account of intricate and oozy channels, and of shoals and breakers which frequently extended far out to sea. The coast which succeeded, that of Sousis (from which Persis is separated by the river Arosis or Oroatis, now the Tâb) was equally difficult and dangerous to navigate, and therefore the fleet no longer crept along the shore, but stood out more into the open sea. At the head of the gulf Sousis bends to westward, and here are the mouths of the Tigris and Euphrates, which appear in those days to have entered the sea by separate channels. It was the intention of Nearkhos to have sailed up the former river, but he passed its mouth unawares, and continued sailing westward till he reached Diridôtis (or Terêdon), an emporium in Babylonia, situated on the Pallacopas branch of the Euphrates. From Diridôtis he retraced his course, and entering the mouth of the Tigris sailed up its stream till he reached the lower end of a great lake (not now existing), through which its current flowed. At the upper end of this lake was a village called Aginis, said to have been 500 stadia distant from Sousa. Nearkhos did not, as has been erroneously supposed by some, sail up the lake to Aginis, but entered the mouth of a river which flows into its south-eastern extremity, called the Pasitigris or Eulæus, the Ulai of the Prophet Daniel, now the Karûn. The fleet proceeded up this river, and came to a final anchor in its stream immediately below a bridge, which continued the highway from Persia to Sousa. This bridge, according to Ritter and Rawlinson, crossed the Pasitigris at a point near the modern village of Ahwaz. Here the fleet and the army were happily reunited. Alexander on his arrival embraced Nearkhos with cordial warmth, and rewarded appropriately the splendid services which he had rendered by bringing the expedition safely through so many hardships and perils to its destination. The date on which the fleet anchored at the bridge is fixed by Vincent for the 24th of February B. C. 325, so that the whole voyage was performed in 146 days, or somewhat less than 5 months.

The following tables show the names, positions, &c., of the different places which occurred on the route taken by the expedition:—

I.

From the Station on the Indus to the Port of Alexander (Karâchi Harbour).

Ancient name.	Modern name.	Distance in Stadia.[32]	Lat. N.	Long. E.
1. Station at Killouta.	Near Lari-Bandar		24° 30′	67° 28′
2. Stoura		100		
3. Kaumana	Khau	30		
4. Koreatis		20		
5. Herma	*Bar in the Indus.*			
6. Krôkala		120		
7. *Mount Eiros*	Manora.			
8. *Is. unnamed.*				
9. The Port of Alexander.	Karâchi		24° 53′	66° 57′

II.

Coast of the Arabies (Sindh).

Length of the Coast from the Indus to the Arabis R.   1000   Stadia.

Actual length in miles English   80

Time taken in its navigation   38   Days.

Ancient name.	Modern name.	Distance in Stadia.	Lat. N.	Long. E.
1. Port of Alexander	Karâchi		24° 53′	66° 57′
2. *Bibakta*				
3. Domai Is.		60	24° 48′	66° 50′
4. Saranga		300	24° 44′	66° 34′
5. Sakala			24° 52′	66° 33′

[32] The Olympic stadium, which was in general use throughout Greece, contained 600 Greek feet = 625 Roman feet, or 606 English feet. The Roman mile contained eight stadia, being about half a stadium less than an English mile. Not a few of the measurements given by Arrian are excessive, and it has therefore been conjectured that he may have used some standard different from the Olympic,—which, however, is hardly probable. See the subject discussed in Smith's Dictionary of Antiquities, S. V. *Stadium.*

6. Morontobara		300	25° 13′	66° 40′
7. *Is. unnamed*				
8. Arabis R.	Puráli R.	120	25° 28′	66° 35′

III.

Coast of Orcitai (Las.)

Length of the coast (Arrian)	1600 Stadia.
Length of the coast (Strabo)	1800 Stadia.
Actual length in miles English	100
Time taken in its navigation	18 Days.

Ancient name.	Modern name.	Distance in Stadia.	Lat. N.	Long. E.
1. Pagala		200	25° 30′	66° 15′
2. Kabana		400	25° 28′	65° 46′
3. Kôkala	NearRâs-Katchari	200	25° 21′	65° 36′
4. Tomêros R.	Maklow or Hingul R.	500	25° 16′	65° 15′
5. Malana	Râs Malan	300	25° 18′	65° 7′

IV.

Coast of the Ikhthyophagoi (Mekran or Beluchistan).

Length of the coast (Arrian)	10000 Stadia.
Length of the coast (Strabo)	7000 Stadia.
Actual length in miles English	480
Time taken in its navigation	90 Days.

Ancient name.	Modern name.	Distance in Stadia.	Lat. N.	Long. E.
1. Bagisara	On Arabah or Hormara Bay	600	25° 12′	64° 31′
2. *Pasira*				
3. Cape unnamed	Râs Arabah		25° 7′	64° 29′
4. Kolta		200	25° 8′	64° 27′
5. Kalama	Kalami R.	600	25° 21′	63° 59′
6. *Karbine Is.*	Asthola or Sânga-dîp			
7. Kissa in *Karbis*		200	25° 22′	63° 37′
8. Cape unnamed	C. Passence		25° 15′	63° 30′
9. Mosarna	Near C. Passence			

Ancient name.	Modern name.	Distance in Stadia.	Lat. N.	Long. E.
10. Balômon		750		
11. Barna		400	25° 12′	63° 10′
12. Dendrobosa	Daram or Duram	200	25° 11′	62° 45′
13. Kôphas	Râs Koppa	400	25° 11′	62° 29′
14. Kuiza	Near Râs Ghunse	800	25° 10′	61° 56′
15. Town unnamed	On Gwattar Bay	500		
16. Cape called Bagia			25° 7′	61° 28′
17. Talmena	On Chaubar Bay	1000	25° 24′	60° 40′
18. Kanasis		400	25° 24	60° 12′
19. Anchorage unnamed.				
20. Kanate	Kungoun	850	25° 25′	59° 15′
21. Taœi or Troisi	Near Sudich River	800	25° 30′	58° 42′
22. Bagasira	Girishk	300	25° 38′	58° 27′
23. Anchorage unnamed		1100		

V.

Coast of Karmania (Moghistan and Laristan).

Length of the coast (Arrian and Strabo)   3,700   Stadia.

Actual length in miles English   296

Time taken in its navigation   19   Days.

Ancient name.	Modern name.	Distance in Stadia.	Lat. N.	Long. E.
1. Anchorage unnamed				
2. Badis	Near Cape Bombarak		25° 47′	57° 48′
3. Anchorage unnamed		800		
4. *Cape Maketa in Arabia*	*Cape Musendom*			
5. Neoptana	Nr. Karun	700	26° 57′	57° 1′
6. Anamis R.	Mînâb R.	100	27° 11′	57° 6′
7. *Organa Is.*	*Ormus or Djerun*			
8. Orakta Is. 2 anchorages	Kishm	300		
9. *Island dist. from it 40 stadia.*	*Angar or Hanjam*			
10. Island 300 stadia from mainland.	Tombo	400	26° 20′	55° 20′
11. *Pylora Is.*	*Polior Is.*		26° 20′	54° 35′

12. Sisidone	Mogos?			
13. Tarsia	C. Djard	300	26° 20′	54° 21′
14. Kataia Is.	Kenn	300	26° 32′	54°

VI.

Coast of Persis (Farsistan).

Length of the Coast	4,400	Stadia.
Actual length in miles English	382	
Time taken in its navigation	31	Days.

Ancient name.	Modern name.	Distance in Stadia.	Lat. N.	Long. E.
1. Ila and Kaikander Is.	Inderabia Island	400	26° 38′	53° 35′
2. Island with Pearl Fishery				
3. Another anchorage here		40		
4. Mount Okhos			26° 59′	53° 20′
5. Apostana		450	27° 1′	52° 55′
6. Bay unnamed	On it is Nabend	400	27° 24′	52° 25′
7. Gôgana at mouth of Areôn R.	Konkan	600	27° 48′	52°
8. Sitakos	Kara-Agach R.	800		
9. Hieratis		750	28° 52′	50° 45′
10. Heratemis R. near it.				
11. Podagron, R.				
12. Mesambria	Near Bushire.		29°	50° 45′
13. Taökê on Granis, R.	Taaug	200	29° 14′	50° 30′
14. Rhogonis, R.		200	29° 27′	50° 29′
15. Brizana, R.		400	29° 57′	50° 15′
16. Arosis or Oroatis, R.	River Tâb.		30°4′	49° 30′

VII.

Coast of Sousis (Khuzistan.)

Length of the Coast	2000	Stadia.
Time taken in its navigation	3	Days.

Ancient name.	Modern name.	Distance in Stadia.	Lat. N.	Long. E.
1. Kataderbis R.		500	30° 16′	49°
2. Margastana Is.				
3. Anchorage unnamed.		600		
4. Diridôtis, the end of the sea voyage.	Near Jebel Sanâm.	900	30° 12′	47° 35′

TRANSLATION.

XVIII. When the fleet formed for Alexander upon the banks of the Hydaspes was now ready, he provided crews for the vessels by collecting all the Phœnikians and all the Kyprians and Egyptians who had followed him in his Eastern campaigns, and from these he selected such as were skilled in seamanship to manage the vessels and work the oars. He had besides in his army not a few islanders familiar with that kind of work, and also natives both of Ionia and of the Hellespont. The following officers he appointed as Commanders of the different galleys[33]: —

Makedonians.

Citizens of Pella.

1. Hephaistiôn, son of Amyntor.

2. Leonnatos, son of Anteas.

3. Lysimakhos, son of Agathoklês.

4. Asklepiodôros, son of Timander.

5. Arkhôn, son of Kleinias.

6. Demonikos, son of Athenaios.

7. Arkhias, son of Anaxidotos.

8. Ophellas, son of Seilênos.

9. Timanthês, son of Pantiadês.

Of Amphipolis.

10. Nearkhos, son of Androtîmos, who wrote a narrative of the voyage.

11. Laomedôn, son of Larikhos.

12. Androsthenês, son of Kallistratos.

---

[33] This list does not specify those officers who performed the voyage, but such as had a temporary command during the passage down the river. The only names which occur afterwards in the narrative are those of Arkhias and Onêsikritos. Nearkhos, by his silence, leaves it uncertain whether any other officers enumerated in his list accompanied him throughout the expedition. The following are known not to have done so: Hephaistion, Leonnatos, Lysimakhos, Ptolemy, Krateros, Attalos and Peukestas. It does not clearly appear what number of ships or men accompanied Nearkhos to the conclusion of the voyage. If we suppose the ships of war only fit for the service, 30 galleys might possibly contain from two to three thousand men, but this estimation is uncertain.

See Vincent, I. 118 sqq.

Of Oresis.

13. Krateros, son of Alexander.

14. Perdikkas, son of Orontes.

Of Eördaia.

15. Ptolemaios, son of Lagos.

16. Aristonous, son of Peisaios.

Of Pydna.

17. Metrôn, son of Epikharmos.

18. Nikarkhidês, son of Simos.

Of Stymphaia.

19. Attalos, son of Andromenês.

Of Mieza.

20. Peukestas, son of Alexander.

Of Alkomenai.

21. Peithôn, son of Krateuas.

Of Aigai.

22. Leonnatos, son of Antipater.

Of Alôros.

23. Pantoukhos, son of Nikolaös.

Of Beroia.

24. Mylleas, son of Zôilos.

All these were Makedonians.

Greeks,—of Larisa:

25. Mêdios, son of Oxynthemis.

Of Kardia.

26. Eumenês, son of Hierônymos.

Of Kôs.

27. Kritoboulos, son of Plato.

Of Magnêsia.

28. Thoas, son of Mênodôros.

29. Maiander, son of Mandrogenês.

Of Teos.

30. Andrôn, son of Kabêlas.

Of Soloi in Cyprus.

31. Nikokleês, son of Pasikratês.

Of Salamis in Cyprus.

32. Nithaphôn, son of Pnutagoras.

A Persian was also appointed as a Trierarch.

33. Bagoas, son of Pharnoukhês.

The Pilot and Master of Alexander's own ship was Onêsikritos of Astypalaia, and the Secretary-General of the fleet Euagoras, the son of Eukleôn, a Corinthian. Nearkhos, the son of Androtîmos, a Kretan by birth, but a citizen of Amphipolis on the Strymôn was appointed as Admiral of the expedition.

When these dispositions had been all completed, Alexander sacrificed to his ancestral gods, and to such as had been indicated by the oracle; also to Poseidôn and Amphitritê and the Nêreids, and to Okeanos himself, and to the River Hydaspês, from which he was setting forth on his enterprise; and to the Akesinês into which the Hydaspês pours its stream, and to the Indus which receives both these rivers. He further celebrated the occasion by holding contests in music and gymnastics, and by distributing to the whole army, rank by rank, the sacrificial victims.

XIX. When all the preparations for the voyage had been made, Alexander ordered Krateros, with a force of horse and foot, to go to one side of the Hydaspês; while Hephaistiôn commanding a still larger force, which included 200 elephants, should march in a parallel line on the other side. Alexander himself had under his immediate command the body of foot guards called the Hypaspists, and all the archers, and what was called the companion-cavalry, — a force consisting in all of 8,000 men. The troops under Krateros and Hephaistiôn marching in advance of the fleet had received instructions where they were to wait its arrival. Philip, whom he had appointed satrap of this region, was despatched to the banks of the Akesinês with another large division, for by this time he had a following of 120,000 soldiers,[34] including those whom he had himself led up from the sea-coast, as well as the recruits enlisted by the agents whom he had deputed to collect an army, when he admitted to his ranks barbarous tribes of all countries in whatever way they might be armed. Then weighing anchor, he sailed down the Hydaspês to its point of junction with the Akesinês. The ships numbered altogether 1800, including the long narrow war galleys, the round-shaped roomy merchantmen, and the transports for carrying horses and provisions to feed the army. But how the fleet sailed down the rivers, and what tribes Alexander conquered in the course of the voyage, and how he was in danger among the Malli,[35] and how he was wounded in their country, and how Peukestas and Leonnatos covered him with their shields when he fell, — all these incidents have been already related in my other work, that which is written in the Attic dialect.[36] My present object is to give an account of <u>the coasting voyage</u> which Nearkhos accomplished with the fleet when starting

[34] So also Plutarch in the Life of Alexander (C. 66) says that in returning from India Alexander had 120,000 foot and 15,000 cavalry.

[35] Sansk. Malava. The name is preserved in the modern Moultan.

[36] Anab. VI. 11.

from the mouths of the Indus he sailed through the great ocean as far as the Persian Gulf, called by some the Red Sea.

XX. Nearkhos himself has supplied a narrative of this voyage, which runs to this effect. Alexander, he informs us, had set his heart on navigating the whole circuit of the sea which extends from India to Persia, but the length of the voyage made him hesitate, and the possibility of the destruction of his fleet, should it be cast on some desert coast either quite harbourless or too barren to furnish adequate supplies; in which case a great stain tarnishing the splendour of his former actions would obliterate all his good fortune. His ambition, however, to be always doing something new and astonishing prevailed over all his scruples. Then arose a difficulty as to what commander he should choose, having genius sufficient for working out his plans, and a difficulty also with regard to the men on ship-board how he could overcome their fear, that in being despatched on such a service they were recklessly sent into open peril. Nearkhos here tells us that Alexander consulted him on the choice of a commander, and that when the king had mentioned one man after another, rejecting all, some because they were not inclined to expose themselves for his sake to danger, others because they were of a timid temper, others because their only thought was how to get home, making this and that objection to each in turn, Nearkhos then proffered his own services in these terms: "I, then, O king, engage to command the expedition, and, under the divine protection, will conduct the fleet and the people on board safe into Persia, if the sea be that way navigable, and the undertaking within the power of man to perform." Alexander made a pretence of refusing the offer, saying that he could not think of exposing any friend of his to the distresses and hazard of such a voyage, but Nearkhos, so far from withdrawing his proposal, only persisted the more in pressing its acceptance upon him. Alexander, it need not be said, warmly appreciated the promptitude to serve him shown by Nearkhos, and appointed him to be commander-in-chief of the expedition. When this became known, it had a great effect in calming the minds of the troops ordered on this service and on the minds of the sailors, since they felt assured that Alexander would never have sent forth Nearkhos into palpable danger unless their lives were to be preserved. At the same time the splendour with which the ships were equipped, and the enthusiasm of the officers vying with each other who should collect the best men, and have his complement most effective, inspired even those who had long hung back with nerve for the work, and a good hope that success would crown the undertaking. It added to the cheerfulness pervading the army that Alexander himself sailed out from both the mouths of the Indus into the open main when he sacrificed victims to Poseidôn and all the other sea-deities, and presented gifts of great magnificence to the sea; and so the men trusting to the immeasurable good fortune which had hitherto attended all the projects of Alexander, believed there was nothing he might not dare—nothing but would to him be feasible.

XXI. When the Etesian winds,[37] which continue all the hot season blowing

[37] The general effect of the monsoon Nearkhos certainly knew; he was a native of Crete, and a resident at Amphipolis, both which lie within the track of the annual or Etesian winds, which commencing from the Hellespont and probably from the Euxine sweep the Egêan sea, and stretching quite across the Mediterranean to the coast of Africa, entered

landward from the sea, making navigation on that coast impracticable, had subsided, then the expedition started on the voyage in the year when Kephisidôros was Archon at Athens, on the 20th day of the month Boëdromion according to the Athenian Kalendar, but as the Makedonians and Asiatics reckon * * in the 11th year of the reign of Alexander.[38] Nearkhos, before putting to sea sacrifices to Zeus the Preserver, and celebrates, as Alexander had done, gymnastic games. Then clearing out of harbour they end the first day's voyage by anchoring in the Indus at a creek called Stoura, where they remain for two days. The distance of this place from the station they had just left was 100 stadia. On the third day they resumed the voyage, but proceeded no further than 30 stadia, coming to an anchor at another creek, where the water was now salt, for the sea when filled with the tide ran up the creek, and its waters even when the tide receded commingled with the river. The name of this place was Kaumana. The next day's course, which was of 20 stadia only, brought them to Koreatis, where they once more anchored in the river. When again under weigh their progress was soon interrupted, for a bar was visible which there obstructed the mouth of the Indus; and the waves were heard breaking with furious roar upon its strand which was wild and rugged. Observing, however, that the bar at a particular part was soft, they made a cutting through this, 5 stadia long, *at low water*, and on the return of the flood-tide carried the ships through by the passage thus formed into the open sea.[39] Then following the winding of the

---

through Egypt to Nubia or Ethiopia. Arrian has accordingly mentioned the monsoon by the name of the Etesian winds; his expression is remarkable, and attended with a precision that does his accuracy credit. These Etesian winds, says he, do not blow from the north in the summer months as with us in the Mediterranean, but from the South. On the commencement of winter, or at latest on the setting of the Pleiades, the sea is said to be navigable till the winter solstice (Anab. VI. 21-1) Vincent I. 43 sq.

[38] The date here fixed by Arrian is the 2nd of October 326 B.C., but the computation now generally accepted refers the event to the year after to suit the chronology of Alexander's subsequent history (see Clinton's F. Hell. II. pp. 174 and 563, 3rd ed.). There was an Archon called Kephisidoros in office in the year B.C. 323-322; so Arrian has here either made a mistake, or perhaps an Archon of the year 326-325 may have died during his tenure of office, and a substitute called Kephisidôros been elected to fill the vacancy. The *lacuna* marked by the asterisks has been supplied by inserting the name of the Makedonian month Dius. The Ephesians adopted the names of the months used by the Makedonians, and so began their year with the month Dius, the first day of which corresponds to the 24th of September. The 20th day of Boedromion of the year B.C. 325 corresponded to the 21st of September.

[39] Regarding the sunken reef encountered by the fleet after leaving Koreatis, Sir Alexander Burnes says: "Near the mouth of the river we passed a rock stretching across the stream, which is particularly mentioned by Nearchus, who calls it *a dangerous rock*, and is the more remarkable since there is not even a stone below Tatta in any other part of the Indus." The rock, he adds, is at a distance of six miles up the Pitti. "It is vain," says Captain Wood in the narrative of his *Journey to the Source of the Oxus*, "in the delta of such a river (as the Indus), to identify existing localities with descriptions handed down to us by the historians of Alexander the Great ... (but) Burnes has, I think, shown that the mouth by which the Grecian fleet left the Indus was the modern *P i t t i*. The 'dangerous rock' of Nearchus completely identifies the spot, and as it is still in existence, without any other within a circle of many miles, we can wish for no stronger evidence." With regard to the canal dug through this rock, Burnes remarks: "The Greek admiral only availed himself of the experience of the people, for it is yet customary among the natives of Sind to dig shallow canals, and leave

coast they ran a course of 120 stadia, and reach Krôkala,[40] a sandy island where they anchored and remained all next day. The country adjoining was inhabited by an Indian race called the Arabies, whom I have mentioned in my longer work, where it is stated that they derive their name from the River Arabis, which flows through their country to the sea, and parts them from the Oreitai.[41] Weighing from Krôkala they had on their right hand a mountain which the natives called Eiros, and on their left a flat island almost level with the sea, and so near the mainland to which it runs parallel that the intervening channel is extremely narrow. Having quite cleared this passage they come to anchor in a well-sheltered harbour, which Nearkhos, finding large and commodious, designated Alexander's Haven. This harbour is protected by an island lying about 2 stadia off from its entrance. It is called Bibakta, and all the country round about Sangada.[42] The existence of the harbour is due altogether to the island which opposes a barrier to the violence of the sea. Here heavy gales blew from seaward for many days without intermission, and Nearkhos fearing lest the barbarians might, some of them, combine to attack and plunder the camp, fortified his position with an enclosure of stones. Here they were obliged to remain for 24 days. The soldiers, we learn from Nearkhos, caught mussels and oysters, and what is called the razor-fish, these being all of an extraordinary size as compared with the sorts found in our own sea.[43] He adds that they

---

the tides or river to deepen them; and a distance of five stadia, or half a mile, would call for not great labour. It is not to be supposed that sandbanks will continue unaltered for centuries, but I may observe that there was a large bank contiguous to the island, between it and which a passage like that of Nearchus might have been dug with the greatest advantage." The same author thus describes the mouth of the Piti:—"Beginning from the westward we have the Pitti mouth, an embouchure of the Buggaur, that falls into what may be called the Bay of Karachi. It has no bar, but a large sandbank, together with an island outside prevent a direct passage into it from the sea, and narrow the channel to about half a mile at its mouth."

[40] All inquirers have agreed in identifying the Kolaka of Ptolemy, and the sandy island of Krokola where Nearchus tarried with his fleet, for one day, with a small island in the bay of Karâchi. Krôkala is further described as lying off the mainland of the Arabii. It was 150 stadia, or 17¼ miles, from the western mouth of the Indus,—which agrees exactly with the relative positions of Karâchi and the mouth of the Ghâra river, if, as we may fairly assume, the present coast-line has advanced five or six miles during the twenty-one centuries that have elapsed since the death of Alexander. The identification is continued by the fact that the district in which Karâchi is situated is called *K a r k a l l a* to this day. Cunningham *Geog. of An. India*, I. p. 306.

[41] The name of the Arabii is variously written,—Arabitæ, Arbii, Arabies, Arbies, Aribes, Arbiti. The name of their river has also several forms,—Arabis, Arabius, Artabis, Artabius. It is now called the *P u r â l i*, the river which flows through the present district of Las into the bay of Soumiyâni. The name of the Oreitai in Curtius is Horitæ. Cunningham identifies them with the people on the Aghor river, whom he says the Greeks would have named Agoritæ or Aoritæ, by the suppression of the guttural, of which a trace still remains in the initial aspirate of 'Horitæ.' Some would connect the name with *H a u r*, a town which lay on the route to Firabaz, in Mekran.

[42] This name Sangada, D'Anville thought, survived in that of a race of noted pirates who infested the shores of the gulf of Kachh, called the *S a n g a d i a n s* or Sangarians.

[43] "The pearl oyster abounds in 11 or 12 fathoms of water all along the coast of Scinde. There was a fishery in the harbour of Kurrachee which had been of some importance in the

had no water to drink but what was brackish.

XXII. As soon as the monsoon ceased they put again to sea, and having run fully 60 stadia came to anchor at a sandy beach under shelter of a desert island that lay near, called Domai.[44] On the shore itself there was no water, but 20 stadia inland it was procured of good quality. The following day they proceeded 300 stadia to Saranga, where they did not arrive till night. They anchored close to the shore, and found water at a distance of about 8 stadia from it. Weighing from Saranga they reach Sakala, a desert place, and anchored. On leaving it they passed two rocks so close to each other that the oar-blades of the galleys grazed both, and after a course of 300 stadia they came to anchor at Morontobara.[45] The harbour here was deep and capacious, and well sheltered all round, and its waters quite tranquil, but the entrance into it was narrow. In the native language it was called Women's Haven, because a woman had been the first sovereign of the place. They thought it a great achievement to have passed those two rocks in safety, for when they were passing them the sea was boisterous and running high. They did not remain in Morontobara, but sailed the day after their arrival, when they had on their left hand an island which sheltered them from the sea, and which lay so near to the mainland that the intervening channel looked as if it had been artificially formed. Its length from one end to the other was 70 stadia.[46] The shore was woody and the island throughout over-grown with trees of every description. They were not able to get fairly through this passage till towards daybreak, for the sea was not only rough, but also shoal, the tide being at ebb. They sailed on continuously, and after a course of 120 stadia anchored at the mouth of the river Arabis, where there was a spacious and very fine haven.[47] The water here was not fit for drinking, for the

days of the native rulers." — *Wanderings of a Naturalist in India*, p. 36.

[44] This island is not known, but it probably lay near the rocky headland of Irus, now called *M a n o r a*, which protects the port of Karâchi from the sea and bad weather.

[45] "The name of Morontobara," says Cunningham, "I would identify with Muâri, which is now applied to the headland of Râs Muâri or Cape Monze, the last point of the Pab range of mountains. *Bâra*, or *Bâri*, means roadstead or haven; and Moranta is evidently connected with the Persian *Mard* a man, of which the feminine is still preserved in Kâśmîrî as *Mahrin* a woman. From the distances given by Arrian, I am inclined to fix it at the mouth of the *B a h a r* rivulet, a small stream which falls into the sea about midway between Cape Monze and Sonmiyâni." *Women's Haven* is mentioned by Ptolemy and Ammianus Marcellinus. There is in the neighbourhood a mountain now called *M o r*, which may be a remnant of the name Morontobari. The channel through which the fleet passed after leaving this place no longer exists, and the island has of course disappeared.

[46] The coast from Karâchi to the Purâli has undergone considerable changes, so that the position of the intermediate places cannot be precisely determined. "From Cape Monze to Sonmiyâni," says Blair, "the coast bears evident marks of having suffered considerable alterations from the encroachments of the sea. We found trees which had been washed down, and which afforded us a supply of fuel. In some parts I saw imperfect creeks in a parallel direction with the coast. These might probably be the vestiges of that narrow channel through which the Greek galleys passed."

[47] Ptolemy and Marcian enumerate the following places as lying between the Indus and the Arabis: Rhizana, Koiamba, Women's Haven, Phagiaura, Arbis. Ptolemy does not mention the Oreitai, but extends the Arabii to the utmost limit of the district assigned to them in Arrian. He makes, notwithstanding, the river Arabia to be the boundary of the Ara-

sea ran up the mouths of the Arabis. Having gone, however, about 40 stadia up the river, they found a pool from which, having drawn water, they returned to the fleet. Near the harbour is an island high and bare, but the sea around it supplied oysters and fish of various kinds.[48] As far as this, the country was possessed by the Arabies, the last Indian people living in this direction; and the parts beyond were occupied by the Oreitai.[49]

XXIII. On weighing from the mouths of the Arabia, they coasted the shores of the Oreitai, and after running 200 stadia reached Pagala,[50] where there was a surf but nevertheless good anchorage. The crew were obliged to remain on board, a party, however, being sent on shore to procure water. They sailed next morning at sunrise, and after a course of about 430 stadia, reached Kabana[51] in the evening, where they anchored at some distance from the shore, which was a desert; the violence of the surf by which the vessels were much tossed preventing them from landing. While running the last course the fleet had been caught in a heavy gale blowing from seaward, when two galleys and a transport foundered. All the men, however, saved themselves by swimming, as the vessels at the time of the disaster were sailing close to the shore. They weighed from Kabana about midnight, and having proceeded 200 stadia arrived at Kôkala, where the vessels *could not be drawn on shore*, but rode at anchor out at sea. As the men, however, had suffered severely by confinement on board,[52] and were very much in want of rest,

bii. His Arabis must therefore be identified not with the *Pârâli*, but with the *Kurmut*, called otherwise the *Rumra* or *Kalami*, where the position of Arrian's Kalama must be fixed. Pliny (vi. 25) places a people whom he calls the Arbii between the Oritae and Karmania, assigning as the boundary between the Arbii and the Oritae the river Arbis.

[48] The *A r a b i s* or *P u r â l i* discharges its waters into the bay of Sonmiyâni. "Sonmiyâni," says Kempthorne, "is a small town or fishing village situated at the mouth of a creek which runs up some distance inland. It is governed by a Sheikh, and the inhabitants appear to be very poor, chiefly subsisting on dried fish and rice. A very extensive bar or sandbank runs across the mouth of this inlet, and none but vessels of small burden can get over it even at high water, but inside the water is deep." The inhabitants of the present day are as badly off for water as their predecessors of old. "Everything," says one who visited the place, "is scarce, even water, which is procured by digging a hole five or six feet deep, and as many in diameter, in a place which was formerly a swamp; and if the water oozes, which sometimes it does not, it serves them that day, and perhaps the next, when it turns quite brackish, owing to the nitrous quality of the earth."

[49] Strabo agrees with Arrian in representing the Oreitai as non-Indian. Cunningham, however, relying on statement made by Curtius, Diodorus and the Chinese pilgrim Hwen Thsang, a most competent observer, considers them to be of Indian origin, for their customs, according to the Pilgrim, were like those of the people of Kachh, and their written characters closely resembled those of India, while their language was only slightly different. The Oreitai as early as the 6th century B.C. were tributary to Darius Hystaspes, and they were still subject to Persia nearly 12 centuries later when visited by Hwen Thsang.—*Geog. of An. Ind.* pp. 304 sqq.

[50] Another form is Pegadæ, met with in Philostratos, who wrote a work on India.

[51] To judge from the distances given, this place should be near the stream now called Agbor, on which is situated *H a r k â n â*. It is probably the Koiamba of Ptolemy.

[52] "In vessels like those of the Greeks, which afforded neither space for motion, nor convenience for rest, the continuing on board at night was always a calamity. When a whole crew was to sleep on board, the suffering was in proportion to the confinement."—Vincent,

Nearkhos allowed them to go on shore, where he formed a camp, fortifying it in the usual manner for protection against the barbarians. In this part of the country Leonnatos, who had been commissioned by Alexander to reduce the Oreitai and settle their affairs, defeated that people and their allies in a great battle, wherein all the leaders and 6,000 men were slain, the loss of Leonnatos, being only 15 of his horse, besides a few foot-soldiers, and *one man of note* Apollophanês, the satrap of the Gedrosians.[53] A full account, however, of those transactions is given in my other work, where it is stated that for this service Leonnatos had a golden crown placed upon his head by Alexander in presence of the Makedonian army. Agreeably to orders given by Alexander, corn had been here collected for the victualling of the vessels, and stores sufficient to last for 10 days were put on board. Here also such ships as had been damaged during the voyage were repaired, while all the mariners that Nearkhos considered deficient in fortitude for the enterprise, he consigned to Leonnatos to be taken on by land, but at the same time he made good his complement of men by taking in exchange others more efficient from the troops under Leonnatos.

XXIV. From this place they bore away with a fresh breeze, and having made good a course of 500 stadia anchored near a winter torrent called the Tomêros, which at its mouth expanded into an estuary.[54] The natives lived on the marshy ground near the shore in cabins close and suffocating. Great was their astonishment when they descried the fleet approaching, but *they were not without courage,* and collecting in arms on the shore, drew up in line to attack the strangers when landing. They carried thick spears about 6 cubits long, not headed with iron, but what was as good, hardened at the point by fire. Their number was about 600, and when Nearkhos saw that they stood their ground prepared to fight, he ordered his vessels to advance, and then to anchor just within bowshot of the shore, for he had noticed that the thick spears of the barbarians were adapted only for close fight, and were by no means formidable as missiles. He then issued his directions: those men that were lightest equipped, and the most active and best at swimming were to swim to shore at a given signal: when any one had swum so far that he could stand in the water he was to wait for his next neighbour, and not advance against the barbarians until a file could be formed of three men deep: that done, they were to rush forward shouting the war-cry. The men selected for this service at once plunged into the sea, and swimming rapidly touched ground, still keeping due order, when forming in file, they rushed to the charge, shouting the war-cry, which was repeated from the ships, whence all the while arrows and missiles from engines were launched against the enemy. Then the barbarians terrified by the glittering arms and the rapidity of the landing, and wounded by the arrows and other missiles, against which they had no protection, being all but entirely naked,

I. p. 209 note.

[53] In another passage of Arrian (Anab. VI. 27, 1,) this Apollophanês is said to have been deposed from his satrapy, when Alexander was halting in the capital of Gedrosia. In the Journal Arrian follows Nearkhos, in the History, Ptolemy or Aristobûlus. — Vincent.

[54] From the distances given, the Tomêros must be identified with the *M a k l o w* or *H i n g a l* river; some would, however, make it the *B h u s â l*. The form of the name in Pliny is *T o m b e r u s*, and in Mela — *T u b e r o*. These authors mention another river in connection with the Tomêros, — the *A r o s a p e s* or *A r u s a c e s*.

fled at once without making any attempt at resistance. Some perished in the ensuing flight, others were taken prisoners, and some escaped to the mountains. Those they captured had shaggy hair, not only on their head but all over their body; their nails resembled the claws of wild beasts, and were used, it would seem, instead of iron for dividing fish and splitting the softer kinds of wood. Things of a hard consistency they cut with sharp stones, for iron they had none. As clothing they wore the skins of wild beasts, and occasionally also the thick skins of the large sorts of fish.[55]

XXV. After this action they draw the ships on shore and repair all that had been damaged. On the 6th day they weighed again, and after a course of 300 stadia reached a place called Malana, the last on the coast, of the Oreitai.[56] In the interior these people dress like the Indians, and use similar weapons, but differ from them in their language and their customs. The length of the coast of the Arabies, measured from the place whence the expedition had sailed, was about 1,000 stadia, and the extent of the coast of the Oreitai 1,600 stadia. Nearkhos mentions that as they sailed along the Indian coast (for the people beyond this are not Indians), their shadows did not fall in the usual direction, for when they stood out a good way to the southward, their shadows appeared to turn and fall southward.[57] Those constellations, moreover, which they had been accustomed to see high in the heavens, were either not visible at all, or were seen just on the verge of the horizon, while the Polar constellations which had formerly been always visible now set and soon afterwards rose again. In this Nearkhos appears to me to assert

---

[55] Similar statements are made regarding this savage race by Curtius IX. 10, 9; Diodôros XVII. 105; Pliny VI. 28; Strabo p. 720; Philostratos V. Ap. III., 57. Cf. Agatharkhides passim. — *Müller.*

[56] Its modern representative is doubtless *R â s   M a l i n*, Malen or Moran.

[57] Such a phenomenon could not of course have been observed at Malana, which is about 2 degrees north of the Tropic, and Nearkhos, as has been already noticed (Introd. p. 155), has on account mainly of this statement been represented as a mendacious writer. Schmieder and Gosselin attempt to vindicate him by suggesting that Arrian in copying his journal had either missed the meaning of this passage, or altered it to bring it into accordance with his own geographical theories. Müller, however, has a better and probably the correct explanation to offer. He thinks that the text of Nearkhos which Arrian used contained passages interpolated from Onêsikritos and writers of his stamp. The interpolations may have been inserted by the Alexandrian geographers, who, following Eratosthenes, believed that India lay between the Tropics. In support of this view it is to be noted that Arrian's account of the shadow occurs in that part of his work where he is speaking of Malana of the Oreitai, and that Pliny (VIII. 75) gives a similar account of the shadows that fall on a mountain of a somewhat similar name in the country of that very people. His words are: *In Indiae gente Oretam Mons est Maleus nomine, juxta quem umbrae aestate in Austrum, hieme in Septemtrionem jaciuntur.* Now Pliny was indebted for his knowledge of Mons Maleus to Baeton, who places it however not in the country of the Oreitai but somewhere in the lower Gangetic region among the Suari and Monedes. It would thus appear that what Baeton had said of *Mount Maleus* was applied to *Malana* of the Oreitai, no doubt on account of the likeness of the two names. Add to this that the expression in the passage under consideration, *for the people beyond this (Malana) are not Indians,* is no doubt an interpolation into the text of the Journal, for it makes the Oreitai to be an Indian people, whereas the Journal had a little before made the Arabies to be the last people of Indian descent living in this direction.

nothing improbable, for at Syênê in Egypt they show a well in which, when the sun is at the Tropic, there is no shadow at noon. In Meroë also objects project no shadow at that particular time. Hence it is probable that the shadow is subject to the same law in India which lies to the south, and more especially in the Indian ocean, which extends still further to the southward.

XXVI. Next to the Oreitai lies Gedrosia,[58] an inland province through which Alexander led his army, but this with difficulty, for the region was so desolate that the troops in the whole course of the expedition never suffered such direful extremities as on this march. But all the particulars relating to this I have set down in my larger work (VI. 22-27). The seaboard below the Gedrosians is occupied by a people culled the Ikhthyophagi, and along this country the fleet now pursued its way. Weighing from Malana about the second watch they ran a course of 600 stadia, and reached Bagisara. Here they found a commodious harbour, and at a distance of 60 stadia from the sea a small town called Pasira, whence the people of the neighbourhood were called Pasirees.[59] Weighing early next morning they had to double a headland which projected far out into the sea, and was high and precipitous. Here having dug wells, and got only a small supply of bad water, they rode at anchor that day because a high surf prevented the vessels approaching the shore. They left this place next day, and sailed till they reached Kolta after a course of 200 stadia.[60] Weighing thence at daybreak they reached Kalama, after a course of 600 stadia, and there anchored.[61] Near the beach was a village around which grew a few palm-trees, the dates on which were still green. There was here an island called Karbinê, distant from the shore about 100 stadia.[62] The villagers

---

[58] This country, which corresponds generally to *M e k r a n*, was called also Kedrosia, Gadrosia, or Gadrusia. The people were an Ârianian race akin to the Arakhosii, Arii, and Drangiani.

[59] Bagisara, says Kempthorne, "is now known by the name of *A r a b a h* or *H o r m a - r a h* Bay, and is deep and commodious with good anchorage, sheltered from all winds but those from the southward and eastward. The point which forms this bay is very high and precipitous, and runs out some distance into the sea. A rather large fishing village is situated on a low sandy isthmus about one mile across, which divides the bay from another.... The only articles of provision we could obtain from the inhabitants were a few fowls, some dried fish, and goats. They grew no kind of vegetable or corn, a few water-melons being the only thing these desolate regions bring forth. Sandy deserts extend into the interior as far as the eye can reach, and at the back of these rise high mountains." The *R h a p u a* of Ptolemy corresponds to the Bagisara or *P a s i r a* of Arrian, and evidently survives in the present name of the bay and the headland of *A r a b a*.

[60] *K o l t a.* —A place unknown. It was situated on the western side of the isthmus which connects *R â s   A r a b a* with the mainland.

[61] A different form is Kaluboi. Situated on the river now called *K a l a m i*, or Kumra, or Kurmut, the Arabis of Ptolemy, who was probably misled by the likeness of the name to Karbis as the littoral district was designated here.

[62] Other forms—*K a r n i n e*, Karmina. The coast was probably called Karmin, if Karmis is represented in *K u r m a t*. The island lying twelve miles off the mouth of the Kalami is now called *A s t o l a* or *S a n g a d i p*, which Kempthorne thus describes:—"Ashtola is a small desolate island about four or five miles in circumference, situated twelve miles from the coast of Mekran. Its cliffs rise rather abruptly from the sea to the height of about 300 feet, and it is inaccessible except in one place, which is a sandy beach about one mile in

by way of showing their hospitality brought presents of sheep and fish to Near-khos, who says that the mutton had a fishy taste like the flesh of sea birds for the sheep fed on fish, there being no grass in the place. Next day they proceeded 200 stadia, and anchored off a shore near which lay a village called Kissa, 30 stadia inland.[63] That coast was however called Karbis. There they found little boats such as might belong to miserably poor fishermen, but the men themselves they saw nothing of, for they had fled when they observed the ships dropping anchor. No corn was here procurable, but a few goats had been left, which were seized and put on board, for in the fleet provisions now ran short. On weighing they doubled a steep promontory, which projected about 150 stadia into the sea, and then put into a well-sheltered haven called Mosarna, where they anchored. Here the natives were fishermen, and here they obtained water.[64]

XXVII. From this place they took on board, Nearkhos says, as pilot of the fleet, a Gedrosian called Hydrakês, who undertook to conduct them as far as Kar-mania.[65] Thenceforth until they reached the Persian Gulf, the voyage was more practicable, and the names of the stations more familiar. Departing from Mosarna at night, they sailed 750 stadia, and reached the coast of Balômon. They touched

---

extent on the northern side. Great quantities of turtle frequent this island for the purpose of depositing their eggs. Nearchus anchored off it, and called it Karnine. He says also that he received hospitable entertainment from its inhabitants, their presents being cattle and fish; but not a vestige of any habitation now remains. The Arabs come to this island, and kill immense numbers of these turtles,—not for the purpose of food, but they traffic with the shell to China, where it is made into a kind of paste, and then into combs, ornaments, &c., in imitation of tortoise-shell. The carcasses caused a stench almost unbearable. The only land animals we could see on the island were rats, and they were swarming. They feed chiefly on the dead turtle. The island was once famous as the rendezvous of the Jowassimee pirates." Vincent quotes Blair to this effect regarding the island:—"We were warned by the natives at Passence that it would be dangerous to approach the island of Asthola, as it was enchanted, and that a ship had been turned into a rock. The superstitious story did not deter us; we visited the island, found plenty of excellent turtle, and saw the rock alluded to, which at a distance had the appearance of a ship under sail. The story was probably told to prevent our disturbing the turtle. It has, however, some affinity to the tale of Nearchus's transport." As the enchanted island mentioned afterwards (chap. xxxi.), under the name of Nosala, was 100 stadia distant from the coast, it was probably the same as Karnine.

[63] Another form of the name is Kysa.

[64] The place according to Ptolemy is 900 stadia distant from the Kalami river, but according to Marcianus 1,300 stadia. It must have been situated in the neighbourhood of Cape Passence. The distances here are so greatly exaggerated that the text is suspected to be corrupt or disturbed. From Mosarna to Kophas the distance is represented as 1,750 stadia, and yet the distance from Cape Passence to Râs *K o p p a* (the Kophas of the text) is barely 500 stadia. According to Ptolemy and Marcian Karmania begins at Mosarna, but according to Arrian much further westward, at Badis near Cape Jask.

[65] "From the name given to this pilot I imagine that he was an inhabitant of Hydri-akos, a town near the bay of Churber or Chewabad.... Upon the acquisition of Hydrakês or the Hydriakan two circumstances occur, that give a new face to the future course of the voyage, one is the very great addition to the length of each day's course; and the other, that they generally weighed during the night: the former depending upon the confidence they acquired by having a pilot on board; and the latter on the nature of the land breeze."—Vincent I., p. 244.

next at Barna, which was 400 stadia distant.[66] Here grew many palm trees, and here was a garden wherein were myrtles and flowers from which the men wove chaplets for their hair.[67] They saw now for the first time cultivated trees, and met with natives in a condition above that of mere savages. Leaving this they followed the winding of the coast, and arrived at Dendrobosa, where they anchor in the open sea.[68] They weighed from this about midnight, and after a course of about 400 stadia gained the haven of Kôphas.[69] The inhabitants were fishermen possessed of small and wretched boats, which they did not manage with oars fastened to a row-lock according to the Grecian manner, but with paddles which they thrust on this side, and on that into the water, like diggers using a spade. They found at this haven plenty of good water. Weighing about the first watch they ran 800 stadia, and put into Kyiza, where was a desert shore with a high surf breaking upon it.[70] They were accordingly obliged to let the ships ride at anchor and take their meal on board. Leaving this they ran a course of 500 stadia, and came to a small town built on an eminence not far from the shore. On turning his eyes in that direction Nearkhos noticed that the land had some appearance of being cultivated, and thereupon addressing Arkhias (who was the son of Anaxidotos of Pella, and sailed in the Commander's galley, being a Makedonian of distinction) pointed out to him that they must take possession of the place, as the inhabitants would not willingly supply the army with food. It could not however be taken by assault, a tedious siege would be necessary, and they were already short of provisions. But the country was one that produced corn as the thick stubble which they saw covering the fields near the shore clearly proved. This proposal being approved of by all, he ordered Arkhias to make a feint of preparing the fleet, all but one ship to sail, while he himself, pretending to be left behind with that ship, approached the

---

[66] This place is called in Ptolemy and Marcianus Badera or Bodera, and may have been situated near the Cape now called Chemaul Bunder. It is mentioned under the form Balara by Philostratos (Vit. Apoll. III. 56), whose description of the place is in close agreement with Arrian's.

[67] τῇσι κυμῇσιν. Another reading, not so good however, is, τῇσι κωμήτῇσιν *for the village women*, but the Greeks were not likely to have indulged in such gallantry. Wearing chaplets in the hair on festive occasions was a common practice with the Greeks. Cf. our author's Anab. V. 2. 8.

[68] In Ptolemy a place is mentioned called Derenoibila, which may be the same as this. The old name perhaps survives in the modern *D a r a m* or Durum, the name of a highland on part of the coast between Cape Passence and Cape Guadel.

[69] The name appears to survive in a cognominal Cape—Râs Coppa. The natives use the same kind of boat to this day; it is a curve made of several small planks nailed or sewn together in a rude manner with cord made from the bark of date trees and called *kair*, the whole being then smeared over with dammer or pitch. — *Kempthorne.*

[70] According to Ptolemy and Marcianus this place lay 400 stadia to the west of the promontory of Alambator (now Râs Gnadel). Some trace of the word may be recognized in *R â s G h u n s e*, which now designates a point of land situated about those parts. Arrian passes Cape Guadel without notice. "We should be reasonably surprised at this," says Vincent (I. 248), "as the doubling of a cape is always an achievement in the estimation of a Greek navigator; but having now a native pilot on board, it is evident he took advantage of the land-breeze to give the fleet an offing. This is clearly the reason why we hear nothing in Arrian of Ptolemy's Alabagium, or Alambateir, the prominent feature of this coast."

town as if merely to view it.

XXVIII. When he approached the walls the inhabitants came out to meet him, bringing a present of tunny-fish broiled in pans (the first instance of cookery among the Ikhthyophagi, although these were the very last of them), accompanied with small cakes and dates. He accepted their offering with the proper acknowledgments, but said he wished to see their town, which he was accordingly allowed to enter. No sooner was he within the gates than he ordered two of his archers to seize the portal by which they had entered, while he himself with two attendants and his interpreter mounting the wall hard by, made the preconcerted signal, on seeing which the troops under Arkhias were to perform the service assigned to them. The Makedonians, on seeing the signal, immediately ran their ships towards land, and without loss of time jumped into the sea. The barbarians, alarmed at these proceedings, flew to arms. Upon this Nearkhos ordered his interpreter to proclaim that if they wished their city to be preserved from pillage they must supply his army with provisions. They replied that they had none, and proceeded to attack the wall, but were repulsed by the archers with Nearkhos, who assailed them with arrows from the summit of the wall. Accordingly, when they saw that their city was taken, and on the point of being pillaged, they at once begged Nearkhos to take whatever corn they had, and to depart without destroying the place. Nearkhos upon this orders Arkhias to possess himself of the gates and the ramparts adjoining, and sends at the same time officers to see what stores were available, and whether these would be all honestly given up. The stores were produced, consisting of a kind of meal made from fish roasted, and a little wheat and barley, for the chief diet of these people was fish with bread added as a relish. The troops having appropriated these supplies returned to the fleet, which then hauled off to a cape *in the neighbourhood* called Bagia, which the natives regarded as sacred to the sun.[71]

XXIX. They weighed from this cape about midnight, and having made good a course of 1,000 stadia, put into Talmena, where they found a harbour with good anchorage.[72] They sailed thence to Kanasis, a deserted town 400 stadia distant, where they find a well ready-dug and wild palm-trees.[73] These they cut down, using the tender heads to support life since provisions had again run scarce. They sailed all day and all night suffering great distress from hunger, and then came to an anchor off a desolate coast. Nearkhos fearing lest the men, if they landed, would in despair desert the fleet, ordered the ships to be moved to a distance from

---

[71] *The little town attacked by Nearchus* lay on Gwattar Bay. The promontory in its neighbourhood called *B a g i a* is mentioned by Ptolemy and Marcianus, the latter of whom gives its distance from Kyiza at 250 stadia, which is but half the distance as given by Arrian. To the west of this was the river Kaudryaces or Hydriaces, the modern Baghwar Dasti or Muhani river, which falls into the Bay of Gwattar.

[72] A name not found elsewhere. To judge by the distance assigned, it must be placed on what is now called Chaubar Bay, on the shores of which are three towns, one being called *T i z*,—perhaps the modern representative of Tisa, a place in those parts mentioned by Ptolemy, and which may have been the Talmena of Arrian.

[73] The name is not found elsewhere. It must have been situated on a bay enclosed within the two headlands Râs Fuggem and Râs Godem.

shore. Weighing from this they ran a course of 850 stadia, and came to anchor at Kanate, a place with an open beach and some water-courses.[74] Weighing again, and making 800 stadia, they reach Taoi, where they drop anchor.[75] The place contained some small and wretched villages, which were deserted by the inhabitants upon the approach of the fleet. Here the men found a little food and dates of the palm-tree, beside seven camels left by the villagers which were killed for food. Weighing thence about daybreak they ran a course of 300 stadia, and came to anchor at Dagasira, where the people were nomadic.[76] Weighing again they sailed all night and all day without intermission, and having thus accomplished a course of 1,100 stadia, left behind them the nation of the Ikhthyophagi, on whose shores they had suffered such severe privations. They could not approach the beach on account of the heavy surf, but rode at anchor out at sea. In navigating the Ikhthyophagi coast the distance traversed was not much short of 10,000 stadia. The people, as their name imports, live upon fish. Few of them, however, are fishermen, and what fish they obtain they owe mostly to the tide at whose reflux they catch them with nets made for this purpose. These nets are generally about 2 stadia long, and are composed of the bark (or fibres) of the palm, which they twine into cord in the same way as the fibres of flax are twined. When the sea recedes, hardly any fish are found among the dry sands, but they abound in the depressions of the surface where the water still remains. The fish are for the most part small, though some are caught of a considerable size, these being taken in the nets. The more delicate kinds they eat raw as soon as they are taken out of the water. The large and coarser kinds they dry in the sun, and when properly dried grind into a sort of meal from which they make bread. This meal is sometimes also used to bake cakes with. The cattle as well as their masters fare on dried fish, for the country has no pastures, and hardly even a blade of grass. In most parts crabs, oysters and mussels add to the means of subsistence. Natural salt is found in the country, * * * from these they make oil.[77] Certain of their communities inhabit deserts where not a tree grows, and where there are not even wild fruits. Fish is their sole means of subsistence. In some few places, however, they sow with grain some patches of land, and eat the produce as a viand of luxury along with the fish which forms the staple of their diet. The better class of the population in building their houses use, instead of wood, the bones of whales stranded on the coast, the broadest bones being employed in the framework of the doors. Poor people, and these are the great majority, construct their dwellings with the backbones of fish.[78]

[74] *K a n a t e* probably stood on the site of the modern *K u n g o u n*, which is near *R â s K a l a t*, and not far from the river *B u n t h*.

[75] Another and the common form is Troisi. The villages of the Taoi must have been where the Sudich river enters the sea. Here Ptolemy places his Kommana or Nommana and his follower Marcian his Ommana. See ante p. 104 note.

[76] The place in Ptolemy is called Agrispolis,—in Marcianus, Agrisa. The modern name is *G i r i s h k*.

[77] Schmieder suggests that instead of the common reading here ἀπὸ τούταν ἔλαιον ποιέουσιν Arrian may have written ἀπὸ Θύννων ε. π. *they make oil from thunnies*, i. e. use the fat for oil.

[78] "This description of the natives, with that of their mode of living and the country they inhabit, is strictly correct even to the present day."—Kempthorne.

XXX. Whales of enormous size frequent the outer ocean, besides other fish larger than those found in the Mediterranean. Nearkhos relates that when they were bearing away from Kyiza, the sea early in the morning was observed to be blown up into the air as if by the force of a whirlwind. The men greatly alarmed enquired of the pilots the nature and cause of this phenomenon, and were informed that it proceeded from the blowing of the whales as they sported in the sea. This report did not quiet their alarm, and through astonishment they let the oars drop from their hands. Nearkhos, however, recalled them to duty, and encouraged them by his presence, ordering the prows of those vessels that were near him to be turned as in a sea-fight towards the creatures as they approached, while the rowers were just then to shout as loud as they could the *alala*, and swell the noise by dashing the water rapidly with the oars. The men thus encouraged on seeing the preconcerted signal advanced to action. Then, as they approached the monsters, they shouted the *alala* as loud as they could bawl, sounded the trumpets, and dashed the water noisily with the oars. Thereupon the whales, which were seen ahead, plunged down terror-struck into the depths, and soon after rose astern, when they vigorously continued their blowing. The men by loud acclamations expressed their joy at this unexpected deliverance, the credit of which they gave to Nearkhos, who had shown such admirable fortitude and judgment.

We learn further, that on many parts of the coast whales are occasionally stranded, being left in shallow water at ebb-tide, and thus prevented from escaping back to sea, and that they are sometimes also cast ashore by violent storms. Thus perishing, their flesh rots away, and gradually drops off till the bones are left bare. These are used by the natives in the construction of their huts, the larger ribs making suitable bearing beams, and the smaller serving for rafters. The jaw-bones make arches for the door-ways, for whales are sometimes five and twenty *orguiæ* (fathoms) in length.[79]

XXXI. When they were sailing along the Ikhthyophagi coast, they were told about an island which was said to be about 100 stadia distant from the mainland, and uninhabited. Its name was Nosala, and it was according to the local tradition sacred to the sun. No one willingly visited this island, and if any one was carried to it unawares, he was never more seen. Nearkhos states that a transport of his fleet, manned with an Egyptian crew, disappeared not far from this island, and that the pilots accounted for their disappearance by saying that they must have landed on the island in ignorance of the danger which they would thereby incur. Nearkhos, however, sent a galley of 30 oars to sail round the island, instructing the men not to land, but to approach as near as they could to the shore, and hail the men, shouting out the name of the captain or any other name they had not forgotten. No one answered to the call, and Nearkhos says that he then sailed in person to the island, and compelled his company much against their will to go on shore. He too landed, and showed that the story about the island was nothing but an empty fable. Concerning this same island he heard also another story, which ran to this effect: it had been at one time the residence of one of the Nereids, whose name, he says,

[79] Strabo (XV. ii. 12, 13) has extracted from Nearkhos the same passage regarding whales. See Nearchi fragm. 25. Cf. Onesikritos (fr. 30) and Orthagoras in Aelian, N. An. XVII. 6; Diodor. XVII. 106; Curtius X. 1, 11.

he could not learn. It was her wont to have intercourse with any man who visited the island, changing him thereafter into a fish, and casting him into the sea. The sun, however, being displeased with the Nereid, ordered her to remove from the island. She agreed to do this, and seek a home elsewhere, but stipulated that she should be cured of her malady. To this condition the sun assented, and then the Nereid, taking pity upon the men whom she had transformed into fish, restored them to their human shape. These men were the progenitors of the Ikhthyophagi, the line of succession remaining unbroken down to the time of Alexander. Now, for my part I have no praise to bestow on Nearkhos for expending so much time and ingenuity on the not very difficult task of proving the falsehood of these stories, for, to take up antiquated fables merely with a view to prove their falsehood, I can only regard as a contemptible piece of folly.[80]

XXXII. To the Ikhthyophagi succeed the Gadrôsii, who occupy a most wretched tract of country full of sandy deserts, in penetrating which Alexander and his army were reduced to the greatest extremities, of which an account is to be found in my other work. But this is an inland region, and therefore when the expedition left the Ikhthyophagi, its course lay along Karmania.[81] Here, when they first drew towards shore, they could not effect a landing, but had to remain all night on board anchored in the deep, because a violent surf spread along the shore and far out to sea. Thereafter the direction of their course changed, and they sailed no longer towards sunset, but turned the heads of the vessels more to the north-west. Karmania is better wooded and produces better fruit than the country either of the Ikhthyophagi or the Oreitai. It is also more grassy, and better supplied with water. They anchor next at Badis, an inhabited place in Karmania, where grew cultivated trees of many different kinds, with the exception of the olive, and where also the soil favoured the growth of the vine and of corn.[82] Weighing thence they ran 800 stadia, and came to an anchor off a barren coast, whence they descried a headland projecting far out into the sea, its nearest extremity being to appearance about a day's sail distant. Persons acquainted with those regions asserted that this cape belonged to Arabia, and was called Maketa, whence cinnamon and other products

----

[80] The story of the Nereid is evidently an Eastern version of the story of the enchantress Kirkê. The island here called Nosala is that already mentioned under the name of Karbine, now Asthola.

[81] *Karmania* extended from Cape Jask to Râs Nabend, and comprehended the districts now called Moghostan, Kirman, and Laristan. Its metropolis, according to Ptolemy, was *Karmana*, now *Kirman*, which gives its name to the whole province. The first port in Karmania reached by the expedition was in the neighbourhood of Cape Jask, where the coast is described as being very rocky, and dangerous to mariners on account of shoals and rocks under water. Kempthorne says: "The cliffs along this part of the coast are very high, and in many places almost perpendicular. Some have a singular appearance, one near Jask being exactly of the shape of a quoin or wedge; and another is a very remarkable peak, being formed by three stones, as if placed by human hands, one on the top of the other. It is very high, and has the resemblance of a chimney."

[82] Badis must have been near where the village of Jask now stands, beyond which was the promontory now called Râs Kerazi or Keroot or Bombarak, which marks the entrance to the Straits of Ormus. This projection is the Cape Karpella of Ptolemy. Badis may be the same as the Kanthatis of this geographer.

were exported to the Assyrians.[83] And from this coast where the fleet was now anchored, and from the headland which they saw projecting into the sea right opposite, the gulf in my opinion (which is also that of Nearkhos) extends up into the interior, and is probably the Red Sea. When this headland was now in view Onesikritos, *the chief pilot*, proposed that they should proceed to explore it, and by so shaping their course, escape the distressing passage up the gulf; but Nearkhos opposed this proposal. Onesikritos, he said, must be wanting in ordinary judgment if he did not know with what design Alexander had sent the fleet on this voyage. He certainly had not sent it, because there were no proper means of conducting the whole army safely by land, but his express purpose was to obtain a knowledge of the coasts they might pass on their voyage, together with the harbours and islets, and to have the bays that might occur explored, and to ascertain whether there were towns bordering on the ocean, and whether the countries, were habitable or desert. They ought not therefore to lose sight of this object, seeing that they were now near the end of their toils, and especially that they were no longer in want of the necessary supplies for prosecuting the voyage. He feared, moreover, since the headland stretched towards the south, lest they should find the country there a parched desert destitute of water and insufferably hot. This argument prevailed, and it appears to me that by this counsel Nearkhos saved the expedition, for all accounts represent this cape and the parts adjacent as an arid waste where water cannot possibly be procured.

XXXIII. On resuming the voyage they sailed close to land, and after making about 700 stadia anchored on another shore called Neoptana.[84] From this they weighed next day at dawn, and after a course of 100 stadia anchored at the mouth of the river Anamis[85] in a country called Harmozeia.[86] Here at last they found a

----

[83] Maketa is now called Cape Mesandum in Oman. It is thus described by Palgrave in the Narrative of his Travels through Central and Eastern Arabia (Vol. II. pp. 316-7). The afternoon was already far advanced when we reached the headland, and saw before us the narrow sea-pass which runs between the farthest rooks of Mesandum and the mainland of the Cape. This strait is called the "Bab" or "gate:" it presents an imposing spectacle, with lofty precipices on either side, and the water flowing deep and black below; the cliffs are utterly bare and extremely well adapted for shivering whatever vessels have the ill luck to come upon them. Hence and from the ceaseless dash of the dark waves, the name of "Mesandum" or "Anvil," a term seldom better applied. But this is not all, for some way out at sea rises a huge square mass of basalt of a hundred feet and more in height sheer above the water; it bears the name of "Salâmah" or "safety," a euphemism of good augury for "danger." Several small jagged peaks, just projecting above the surface, cluster in its neighbourhood; these bear the endearing name of "Benât Salâmah," or "Daughters of Salamah."

[84] This place is not mentioned elsewhere, but must have been situated somewhere in the neighbourhood of the village of Karun.

[85] The *A n a m i s*, called by Pliny the Ananis, and by Ptolemy and Mela the Andanis, is now the Minâb or Ibrahim River.

[86] Other forms—Hormazia, Armizia regio. The name was transferred from the mainland to the island now called *O r m u s*, when the inhabitants fled thither to escape from the Moghals. It is called by Arrian *O r g a n a* (chap. xxxvii.) The Arabians called it Djerun, a name which it continued to bear up to the 12th century. Pliny mentions an island called Oguris, of which perhaps Djerun is a corruption. He ascribes to it the honour of having been the birthplace of Erythrés. The description, however, which he gives of it is more ap-

hospitable region, one which was rich in every production except only the olive. Here accordingly they landed, and enjoyed a welcome respite from their many toils—heightening their pleasure by calling to remembrance what miseries they had suffered at sea and in the Ikhthyophagi country, where the shores were so sterile, and the natives so brute-like, and where they had been reduced to the last extremities of want. Here, also, some of them in scattered parties, leaving the encampment on the shore, wandered inland searching for one thing and another that might supply their several requirements. While thus engaged, they fell in with a man who wore a Greek mantle, and was otherwise attired as a Greek and spoke the Greek language. Those who first discovered him declared that tears started to their eyes, so strange did it appear, after all they had suffered, to see once more a countryman of their own, and to hear the accents of their native tongue. They asked him whence he came, and who he was. He replied that he had straggled from the army of Alexander, and that the army led by Alexander in person was not far off. On hearing this they hurry the man with shouts of tumultuous joy to the presence of Nearkhos, to whom he repeated all that he had already said, assuring him that the army and the king were not more than a 5 days' march distant from the sea. The Governor of the province, he added, was on the spot, and he would present him to Nearkhos, and he presented him accordingly. Nearkhos consulted this person regarding the route he should take in order to reach the king, and then they all went off, and made their way to the ships. Early next morning the ships by orders of Nearkhos were drawn on shore, partly for repair of the damages which some of them had suffered on the voyage, and partly because he had resolved to leave here the greater part of his army. Having this in view, he fortified the roadstead with a double palisade, and also with an earthen rampart and a deep ditch extending from the banks of the river to the dockyard where the ships were lying.

XXXIV. While Nearkhos was thus occupied, the Governor being aware that Alexander was in great anxiety about the fate of this expedition, concluded that he would receive some great advantage from Alexander should he be the first to apprize him of the safety of the fleet and of the approaching visit of Nearkhos. Accordingly he hastened to Alexander by the shortest route, and announced that Nearkhos was coming from the fleet to visit him. Alexander, though he could scarcely believe the report, nevertheless received the tidings with all the joy that might have been expected.

Day after day, however, passed without confirmation of the fact, till Alexander, on comparing the distance from the sea with the date on which the report had reached him, at last gave up all belief in its truth, the more especially as several of the parties which he had successively despatched to find Nearkhos and escort him

plicable to the island called by Arrian (chap. xxxvii.) Oârakta (now Kishm) than to Ormus. Arrian's description of Harmozia is still applicable to the region adjacent to the Mînâb. "It is termed," says Kempthorne, "the Paradise of Persia. It is certainly most beautifully fertile, and abounds in orange groves, orchards containing apples, pears, peaches, and apricots, with vineyards producing a delicious grape, from which was made at one time a wine called Amber rosolia, generally considered the white wine of Kishma; but no wine is made here now." The old name of Kishma—Oârakta—is preserved in one of its modern names, Vrokt or Brokt.

to the camp, had returned without him, after going a short distance, and meeting no one, while others who had prosecuted the search further, and failed to find Nearkhos and his company were still absent. He therefore ordered the Governor into confinement for having brought delusive intelligence and rendered his vexation more acute by the disappointment of his hopes, and indeed his looks and perturbation of mind plainly indicated that he was pierced to the heart with a great grief. Meanwhile, however, one of the parties that had been despatched in search of Nearkhos, and his escort being furnished with horses and waggons for their accommodation, fell in on the way with Nearkhos and Arkhias, who were followed by five or six attendants. At first sight they recognized neither the admiral himself nor Arkhias, so much changed was their appearance, their hair long and neglected, their persons filthy, encrusted all over with brine and shrivelled, their complexion sallow from want of sleep and other severe privations. On their asking where Alexander was, they were told the name of the place. Arkhias then, perceiving who they were, said to Nearkhos—"It strikes me, Nearkhos, these men are traversing the desert by the route we pursue, for no other reason than because they have been sent to our relief. True, they did not know us, but that is not at all surprising, for our appearance is so wretched that we are past all recognition. Let us tell them who we are, and ask them why they are travelling this way." Nearkhos, thinking he spoke with reason, asked the men whither they were bound. They replied that they were searching for Nearkhos and the fleet. "Well! I am Nearkhos," said the admiral, "and this man here is Arkhias. Take us under your conduct, and we will report to Alexander the whole history of the expedition."

XXXV. They were accordingly accommodated in the waggons, and conducted to the camp. Some of the horsemen, however, wishing to be the first to impart the news, hastened forward, and told Alexander that Nearkhos himself, and Arkhias with him, and five attendants, would soon arrive, but to enquiries about the rest of the people in the expedition they had no information to give. Alexander, concluding from this that all the expedition had perished except this small band, which had been unaccountably saved, did not so much feel pleasure for the preservation of Nearkhos and Arkhias as distress for the loss of his whole fleet. During this conversation Nearkhos and Arkhias arrived. It was not without difficulty Alexander after a close scrutiny recognized who the hirsute, ill-clad men who stood before him were, and being confirmed by their miserable appearance in his belief that the expedition had perished, he was still more overcome with grief. At length he held out his hand to Nearkhos, and leading him apart from his attendants and his guards he burst into tears, and wept for a long time. Having, after a good while, recovered some composure, "Nearkhos!" he says, "since you and Arkhias have been restored to me alive, I can bear more patiently the calamity of losing all my fleet; but tell me now, in what manner did the vessels and my people perish." "O my king!" replied Nearkhos, "the ships are safe and the people also, and we are here to give you an account of their preservation." Tears now fell much faster from his eyes than before, but they were tears of joy for the salvation of his fleet which he had given up for lost. "And where are now my ships," he then enquired. "They are drawn upon shore," replied Nearkhos, "on the beach of the river Anamis for repairs." Upon this Alexander, swearing by Zeus of the Greeks and Ammon of the

Libyans, declared that he felt happier at receiving these tidings than in being the conqueror of all Asia, for, had the expedition been lost, the blow to his peace of mind would have been a counterpoise to all the success he had achieved.

XXXVI. But the Governor whom Alexander had put into confinement for bringing intelligence that appeared to be false, seeing Nearkhos in the camp, sunk on his knees before him, and said: "I am the man who brought to Alexander the news of your safe arrival. You see how I am situated." Nearkhos interceded with Alexander on his behalf, and he was then liberated. Alexander next proceeded to offer a solemn sacrifice in gratitude for the preservation of his fleet unto Zeus the Preserver, and Heraklês, and Apollo the Averter of Destruction, and unto Poseidôn, and every other deity of ocean. He celebrated likewise a contest in gymnastics and music, and exhibited a splendid procession wherein a foremost place was assigned to Nearkhos. Chaplets were wreathed for his head, and flowers were showered upon him by the admiring multitude. At the end of these proceedings the king said to Nearkhos, "I do not wish you, Nearkhos, either to risk your life or expose yourself again to the hardships of sea-voyaging, and I shall therefore send some other officer to conduct the expedition onward to Sousa." But Nearkhos answered, and said: "It is my duty, O king! as it is also my desire, in all things to obey you, but if your object is to gratify me in some way, do not take the command from me until I complete the voyage by bringing the ships in safety to Sousa. I have been trusted to execute that part of the undertaking in which all its difficulty and danger lay; transfer not, then, to another the remaining part, which hardly requires an effort, and that, too, just at the time when the glory of final success is ready to be won." Alexander scarcely allowed him to conclude his request, which he granted with grateful acknowledgment of his services.[87] Then he sent him down again to the coast with only a small escort, believing that the country through which he would pass was friendly. He was not permitted however to pursue his way to the coast without opposition, for the barbarians, resenting the action of Alexander in deposing their satrap, and gathered in full force and seized all the strongholds of Karmania before Tlepolemos, the newly appointed Governor, had yet succeeded in fully establishing his authority.[88] It happened therefore that several times in the course of a day Nearkhos encountered bands of the insurgents with whom he had to do battle. He therefore hurried forward without lingering by the way, and reached the coast in safety, though not without severe toil and difficulty. On arriving he sacrificed to Zeus the Preserver, and celebrated gymnastic games.

XXXVII. These pious rites having been duly performed, they again put to sea, and, after passing a desolate and rocky island, arrived at another island, where they anchored. This was one of considerable size and inhabited, and 300 stadia distant from Harmozeia, the harbour which they had last left. The desert island was called Organa, and that where they anchored Oarakta.[89] It produced vines,

[87] Diodôros (XVII. 106) gives quite a different account of the visit of Nearkhos to Alexander.

[88] The preceding satrap was Sibyrtios, the friend of Megasthenês. He had been transferred to govern the Gadrosians and the Arakhotians.

[89] As stated in Note 64, Organa is now *Ormuz*, and Oarakta, *Kishm*. Ormuz, once so renowned for its wealth and commerce, that it was said of it by its Portuguese occupants,

palm-trees, and corn. Its length is 800 stadia. Mazênês, the chief of this island, accompanied them all the way to Sousa, having volunteered to act as pilot of the fleet. The natives of the island professed to point out the tomb of the very first sovereign of the country, whose name they said was Erythrês, after whom the sea in that part of the world was called the Erythræan.[90] Weighing thence their course lay along the island, and they anchored on its shores at a place whence another island was visible at a distance of about 40 stadia. They learned that it was sacred to Poseidon, and inaccessible.[91] Next morning, as they were putting out to sea, the ebb-tide caught them with such violence that three of the galleys were stranded on the beach, and the rest of the fleet escaped with difficulty from the surf into deep water. The stranded vessels were however floated off at the return of the tide, and the day after rejoined the fleet. They anchored at another island distant from the mainland somewhere about 300 stadia, after running a course of 400 stadia. Towards daybreak they resumed the voyage, passing a desert island which lay on their left, called Pylora, and anchored at Sisidone, a small town which could supply nothing but water and fish.[92] Here again the natives were fish eaters, for

---

that if the world were a golden ring, Ormuz would be the diamond signet, is now in utter decay. "I have seen," says Palgrave (II. 319), "the abasement of Tyre, the decline of Surat, the degradation of Goa: but in none of those fallen seaports is aught resembling the utter desolation of Ormuz." A recent traveller in Persia (Binning) thus describes the coast: "It presents no view but sterile, barren, and desolate chains of rocks and hills: and the general aspect of the Gulf is dismal and forbidding. Moore's charming allusions to Oman's sea, with its 'banks of pearl and palmy isles' are unfortunately quite visionary; for uglier and more unpicturesque scenery 1 never beheld." — *Two Years' Travel in Persia*, I. pp. 136, 137.

[90] For the legend of Erythrês see Agatharkhides De Mari Eryth. I. 1-4 and Strabo XVI. iv. 20. The Erythræan Sea included the Indian Ocean, the Persian Gulf, and the Red Sea, the last being called also the Arabian Gulf, when it was necessary to distinguish it from the Erythræan in general. It can hardly be doubted that the epithet *Erythræan* (which means *red*, Greek εϱυθϱος) first designated the Arabian Gulf or Red Sea, and was afterwards extended to the seas beyond the Straits by those who first explored them. The Red Sea was so called because it washed the shores of Arabia, called *the Red Land* (Edom), in contradistinction to Egypt, called *the Black Land* (Kemi), from the darkness of the soil deposited by the Nile. Some however thought that it received its name from the quantity of red coral found in its waters, especially along the eastern shores, and Strabo says (loc. cit.): "Some say that the sea is red from the colour arising from reflexion either from the sun, which is vertical, or from the mountains, which are red by being scorched with intense heat; for the colour it is supposed may be produced by both of these causes. Ktesias of Knidos speaks of a spring which discharges into the sea a red and ochrous water." — Cf. Eustath. Comment. 38.

[91] This island is that now called *A n g a r*, or *H a n j a m*, to the south of Kishm. It is described as being nearly destitute of vegetation and uninhabited. Its hills, of volcanic origin, rise to a height of 300 feet. The other island, distant from the mainland about 300 stadia, is now called the Great Tombo, near which is a smaller island called Little Tombo. They are low, flat, and uninhabited. They are 25 miles distant from the western extremity of Kishm.

[92] The island of *P y l o r a* is that now called Polior. *S i s i d o n e* appears in other forms — Prosidodone, pro-Sidodone, pros Sidone, pros Dodone. Kempthorne thought this was the small fishing village now called *M o g o s*, situated in a bay of the same name. The name may perhaps be preserved in the name of a village in the same neighbourhood, called Dnan Tarsia — now *R â s - e l - D j a r d* — described as high and rugged, and of a reddish colour.

the soil was utterly sterile. Having taken water on board, they weighed again, and having run 300 stadia, anchored at Tarsia, the extremity of a cape which projects far into the sea. The next place of anchorage was Kataia, a desert island, and very flat.[93] It was said to be sacred to Hermês and Aphroditê. The length of this course was 300 stadia. To this island sheep and goats are annually sent by the people of the adjoining continent who consecrate them to Hermês and Aphroditê. These animals were to be seen running about in a wild state, the effect of time and the barren soil.

XXXVIII. Karmania extends as far as this island, but the parts beyond appertain to Persia. The extent of the Karmanian coast was 3,700 stadia.[94] The people of this province live like the Persians, on whom they border, and they have similar weapons and a similar military system. When the fleet left the sacred island, its course lay along the coast of Persis, and it first drew to land at a place called Ila, where there is a harbour under cover of a small and desert island called Kaikander.[95] The distance run was 400 stadia. Towards daybreak they came to another island which was inhabited, and anchored thereon. Nearkhos notices that there is here a fishery for pearl as there is in the Indian Sea.[96] Having sailed along the shores of the promontory in which this island terminates, a distance of about 40 stadia, they came to an anchor upon its shores. The next anchorage was in the vicinity of a lofty hill called Okhos, where the harbour was well sheltered and the inhabitants were fishermen.[97] Weighing thence they ran a course of 400 stadia, which brought them to Apostana, where they anchored. At this station they saw a great many boats, and learned that at a distance of 60 stadia from the shore there was a village. From Apostana they weighed at night, and proceeded 400 stadia to a bay, on the borders of which many villages were to be seen. Here the fleet an-

---

[93] *Kataia* is now the island called *Kaes* or *Kenn*. Its character has altered, being now covered with dwarf trees, and growing wheat and tobacco. It supplies ships with refreshment, chiefly goats and sheep and a few vegetables. "At morning," says Binning (I. 137), "we passed Polior, and at noon were running along the South side of the Isle of Keesh, called in our maps Kenn; a fertile and populous island about 7 miles in length. The inhabitants of this, as well as of every other island in the Gulf, are of Arab blood — for every true Persian appears to hate the very sight of the sea."

[94] The boundary between Karmania and Persis was formed by a range of mountains opposite the island of *Kataia*. Ptolemy, however, makes Karmania extend much further, to the river *Bagradas*, now called the *Naban* or *Nabend*.

[95] *Kaikander* has the other forms — Kekander, Kikander, Kaskandrus, Karkundrus, Karskandrus, Sasækander. This island, which is now called *Inderabia*, or *Andaravia*, is about four or five miles from the mainland, having a small town on the north side, where is a safe and commodious harbour. The other island mentioned immediately after is probably that now called Busheab. It is, according to Kempthorne, a low, flat island, about eleven miles from the mainland, containing a small town principally inhabited by Arabs, who live on fish and dates. The harbour has good anchorage even for large vessels.

[96] The pearl oyster is found from Ras Musendom to the head of the Gulf. There are no famed banks on the Persian side, but near Bushire there are some good ones.

[97] *Apostana* was near a place now called *Schevar*. It is thought that the name may be traced in *Dahra Ahbân*, an adjacent mountain ridge of which Okhos was probably the southern extremity.

chored under the projection of a cape which rose to a considerable height.[98] Palm-trees and other fruit-bearing trees similar to those of Greece, adorned the country round. On weighing thence they sailed in a line with the coast, and after a course of somewhere about 600 stadia reached Gôgana, which was an inhabited place, where they anchored at the mouth of a winter torrent called the Areôn. It was difficult to anchor, for the approach to the mouth of the river was by a narrow channel, since the ebbing of the tide had left shoals which lay all round in a circle.[99] Weighing thence they gained, after running as many as 800 stadia, the mouth of another river called the Sitakos, where also it was troublesome to anchor. Indeed all along the coast of Persis the fleet had to be navigated through shoals and breakers and oozy channels. At the Sitakos they took on board a large supply of provisions, which under orders from the king had been collected expressly for the fleet. They remained at this station one-and-twenty days in all, occupied in repairing and kareening the ships, which had been drawn on shore for the purpose.[100]

XXXIX. Weighing thence they came to an inhabited district with a town called Hieratis, after accomplishing a distance of 750 stadia. They anchored in a canal which drew its waters from a river and emptied into the sea, and was called Heratemis.[101] Weighing next morning about sunrise, and sailing by the shore, they reached a winter torrent called the Padargos, where the whole place was a peninsula, wherein were many gardens and all kinds of trees that bear fruit. The name of the place was Mesambria.[102] Weighing from Mesambria and running a course of about 200 stadia, they reach Taôkê on the river Granis, and there anchor. Inland from this lay a royal city of the Persians, distant from the mouths of the river about 200 stadia.[103] We learn from Nearkhos that on their way to Taôkê a stranded whale

---

[98] This bay is that on which *N a b a n* or *N a b e n d* is now situated. It is not far from the river called by Ptolemy the Bagradas. The place abounds with palm-trees as of old.

[99] *G ô g a n a* is now *K o n k a n* or *K o n a u n*. The bay lacks depth of water; a stream still falls into it—the Areôn of the text. To the north-west of this place in the interior lay *P a s a r g a d a*, the ancient capital of Persia, and the burial-place of Kyros, in the neighbourhood of Murghâb, a place to the N. E. of Shiraz (30° 24' N. 56° 29' E.).

[100] The Sitakos has been identified with the Kara Agach, Mand, Mund or Kakee river, which has a course of 300 miles. Its source is near Kodiyan, which lies N. W. of Shiraz. At a part of its course it is called the Kewar River. The meaning of its name is *black wood*. In Pliny it appears as the Sitioganus. *Sitakon* was probably the name as Nearkhos heard it pronounced, as it frequently happens that when a Greek writer comes upon a name like an oblique case in Greek, he invents a nominative for it. With regard to the form of the name in Pliny, 'g' is but a phonetic change instead of 'k'. The 'i' is probably an error in transcription for 't'. The Sitakos is probably the Brisoana of Ptolemy, which can have no connexion with the later-mentioned Brizana of our author. See *Report on the Persian Gulf* by Colonel Ross, lately issued. Pliny states that from the mouth of the Sitioganus an ascent could be made to Pasargada, in seven days; but this is manifestly an error.

[101] The changes which have taken place along the coast have been so considerable that it is difficult to explain this part of the narrative consistently with the now existing state of things.

[102] The peninsula, which is 10 miles in length and 3 in breadth, lies so low that at times of high tide it is all but submerged. The modern *A b u - S h a h r* or *B u s h i r* is situated on it.

[103] Nearkhos, it is probable, put into the mouth of the river now called by some the

had been observed from the fleet, and that a party of the men having rowed along-side of it, measured it and brought back word that it had a length of 50 cubits. Its skin, they added, was clad with scales to a depth of about a cubit, and thickly clustered over with parasitic mussels, barnacles, and seaweed. The monster, it was also noticed, was attended by a great number of dolphins, larger than are ever seen in the Mediterranean. Weighing from Taôkê they proceeded to Rhogonis, a winter torrent, where they anchored in a safe harbour.[104] The course thither was one of 200 stadia. Weighing thence, and running 400 stadia, they arrived at another win-ter torrent, called Brizana, where they land and form an encampment. They had here difficulty in anchoring because of shoals and breakers and reefs that showed their heads above the sea. They could therefore enter the roads only when the tide was full; when it receded, the ships were left high and dry.[105] They weighed with the next flood tide, and came to anchor at the mouth of a river called the Arosis, the greatest, according to Nearkhos, of all the rivers that in the course of his voyage fell into the outer ocean.[106]

XL. The Arosis marks the limit of the possessions of the Persians, and divides them from the Susians. Above the Susians occurs an independent race called the Uxians, whom I have described in my other work (*Anab*. VII. 15, 3) as robbers. The length of the Persian coast is 4,400 stadia. Persis, according to general report, has three different climates,[107] for that part of it which lies along the Erythræan sea, is sandy and barren from the violence of the heat, while the part which succeeds enjoys a delightful temperature, for there the mountains stretch towards the pole and the North wind, and the region is clothed with verdure and has well-watered meadows, and bears in profusion the vine and every fruit else but the olive, while it blooms with gardens and pleasure parks of all kinds, and is permeated with crystal streams and abounds with lakes, and lake and stream alike are the haunts of every variety of water-fowl, and it is also a good country for horses and other

---

K i s h t, by others the Boshavir. A town exists in the neighbourhood called *G r a* or *G r a n*, which may have received its name from the Granis. The royal city (or rather palace), 200 stadia distant from this river, is mentioned by Strabo, xv. 3, 3, as being situate on the coast. Ptolemy does not mention the Granis. He makes Taökê to be an inland town, and calls all the district in this part Taôkênê. Taokê may be the Touag mentioned by Idrisi, which is now represented by Konar Takhta near the Kisht.

[104] *R h o g o n i s .* —It is written Rhogomanis by Ammianus Marcellinus, who men-tions it as one of the four largest rivers in Persia, the other three being the Vatrachitis, Briso-ana, and Bagrada. It is the river at the mouth of which is Bender-Righ or Regh, which is considered now as in the days of Nearkhos to be a day's sail from Bushire.

[105] "The measures here are neglected in the Journal, for we have only 800 stadia specified from Mesambria to Brizana, and none from Brizana to the Arosis; but 800 stadia are short of 50 miles, while the real distance from Mesambria (Bushir) to the Arosis with the winding of the coast is above 140. In these two points we cannot be mistaken, and therefore, besides the omission of the interval between Brizana and the Arosis, there must be some defect in the Journal for which it is impossible now to account."—Vincent, 1. p. 405.

[106] Another form of the name of this river is the Aroatis. It answers to the Zarotis of Pliny, who states that the navigation at its mouth was difficult, except to those well ac-quainted with it. It formed the boundary between Persis and Susiana. The form Oroatis corresponds to the Zend word *aurwat* 'swift.' It is now called the Tâb.

[107] On this point compare Strabo, bk. xv. 3, 1.

yoke cattle, being rich in pasture, while it is throughout well-wooded and well-stocked with game. The part, however, which lies still further to the North is said to be bleak and cold, and covered with snow, so that, as Nearkhos tells us, certain ambassadors from the Euxine Sea, after a very brief journey, met Alexander marching forward to Persis, whereat Alexander being greatly surprised, they explained to him how very inconsiderable the distance was.[108] 1 have already stated that the immediate neighbours to the Susians are the Uxians, just as the Mardians, a race of robbers, are next neighbours to the Persians, and the Kossaeans to the Medes. All these tribes Alexander subdued, attacking them in the winter time when their country was, as they imagined, inaccessible. He then founded cities to reclaim them from their wandering life, and encouraged them to till their lands and devote themselves to agriculture. At the same time he appointed magistrates armed with the terrors of the law to prevent them having recourse to violence in the settlement of their quarrels. On weighing from the Arosis the expedition coasted the shores of the Susians. The remainder of the voyage, Nearkhos says, he cannot describe with the same precision; he can but give the names of the stations and the length of the courses, for the coast was full of shoals and beset with breakers which spread far out to sea, and made the approach to land dangerous. The navigation thereafter was of course almost entirely restricted to the open sea. In mentioning their departure from the mouth of the river where they had encamped on the borders of Persis, he states that they took there on board a five days' supply of water, as the pilots had brought to their notice that none could be procured on the way.

XLI. A course of 500 stadia having been accomplished, their next anchorage was in an estuary, which swarmed with fish, called Kataderbis, at the entrance of which lay an island called Margastana.[109] They weighed at daybreak, the ships sailing out in single file through shoals. The direction of the shoal was indicated by stakes fixed both on the right and the left side, just as posts are erected as signals of danger in the passage between the island of Leukadia and Akarnania to prevent vessels grounding on the shoals. The shoals of Leukadia, however, are of firm sand, and it is thus easy to float off vessels should they happen to strand, but in this passage there is a deep mud on both sides of such tenacity that if vessels once touched the bottom, they could not by any appliances be got off; for, if they thrust poles into the mud to propel the vessels, these found no resistance or support, and the people who got overboard to ease them off into navigable water found no footing, but sunk in the mud higher than the waist. The fleet proceeded 600 stadia, having such difficulties of navigation to contend with, and then came to an anchor, each crew remaining in their own vessel, and taking their repast on board. From this anchorage they weighed in the night, sailing on in deep water till about the close of the ensuing day, when, after completing a course of 900 stadia, they dropped anchor at the mouth of the Euphrates near a town in Babylonia called Diridôtis—the emporium of the sea-borne trade in frankincense and all the other

---

[108] It has been conjectured that the text here is imperfect. Schmieder opines that the story about the ambassadors is a fiction.

[109] The bay of Kataderbis is that which receives the streams of the *M e n s u r e h* and *D o r a k*; at its entrance lie two islands, Bunah and Deri, one of which is the Margastana of Arrian.

fragrant productions of Arabia.[110] The distance from the mouth of the Euphrates up stream to Babylon is, according to Nearkhos, 3,300 stadia.

XLII. Here intelligence having been received that Alexander was marching towards Sousa, they retraced their course from Diridôtis so as to join him by sailing up the Pasitigris. They had now Sousis on their left hand, and were coasting the shores of a lake into which the Tigris empties itself, a river, which flowing from Armenia past Nineveh, a city once of yore great and flourishing, encloses between itself and the Euphrates the tract of country which from its position between the two rivers is called Mesopotamia. It is a distance of 600 stadia from the entrance into the lake up to the river's mouth at Aginis, a village in the province of Sousis, distant from the city of Sousa 500 stadia. The length of the voyage along the coast of the Sousians to the mouth of the Pasitigris was 2,000 stadia.[111] Weighing from the mouth of this river they sailed up its stream through a fertile and populous country, and having proceeded 150 stadia dropped anchor, awaiting the return of certain messengers whom Nearkhos had sent off to ascertain where the king was. Nearkhos then presented sacrifices to the gods their preservers, and celebrated games, and full of gladness were the hearts of all that had taken part in the expedi-

---

[110] *D i r i d ô t i s* is called by other writers Terêdon, and is said to have been founded by Nabukhodonosor. Mannert places it on the island now called *B u b i a n*; Colonel Chesney, however, fixes its position at *J e b e l   S a n â m*, a gigantic mound near the Pallacopas branch of the Euphrates, considerably to the north of the embouchure of the present Euphrates. Nearkhos had evidently passed unawares the stream of the Tigris and sailed too far westward. Hence he had to retrace his course, as mentioned in the next chapter.

[111] This is the Eulæus, now called the *K a r û n*, one arm of which united with the Tigris, while the other fell into the sea by an independent mouth. It is the *U l a i* of the prophet Daniel. *Pas* is said to be an old Persian word, meaning *small*. By some writers the name *P a s i t i g r i s* was applied to the united stream of the Tigris and Euphrates, now called the *S h a t - e l - A r a b*. The courses of the rivers and the conformation of the country in the parts here have all undergone great changes, and hence the identification of localities is a matter of difficulty and uncertainty. The following extract from Strabo will illustrate this part of the narrative:—

Polycletus says that the *C h o a s p e s*, and the *E u l æ u s*, and the *T i g r i s* also enter a lake, and thence discharge themselves into the sea; that on the side of the lake is a mart, as the rivers do not receive the merchandize from the sea, nor convey it down to the sea, on account of dams in the river, purposely constructed; and that the goods are transported by land, a distance of 800 stadia, to Susis: according to others, the rivers which flow through Susis discharge themselves by the intermediate canals of the Euphrates into the single stream of the Tigris, which on this account has at its mouth the name of Pasitigris. According to Nearchus, the sea-coast of Susis is swampy, and terminates at the river Euphrates; at its mouth is a village which receives the merchandize from Arabia, for the coast of Arabia approaches close to the mouths of the Euphrates and the Pasitigris; the whole intermediate space is occupied by a lake which receives the Tigris. On sailing up the Pasitigris 150 stadia is a bridge of rafts leading to Susa from Persis, and is distant from Susa 60 (600?) stadia; the Pasitigris is distant from the Oroatis about 2,000 stadia; the ascent through the lake to the mouth of the Tigris is 600 stadia; near the mouth stands the Susian village Aginis, distant from Susa 500 stadia; the journey by water from the mouth of the Euphrates up to Babylon, through a well-inhabited tract of country, is a distance of more than 3,000 stadia.—Book xv. 3, *Bohn's trans.*

tion. The messengers having returned with tidings that Alexander was approaching, the fleet resumed its voyage up the river, and anchored near the bridge by which Alexander intended to lead his army to Sousa. In that same place the troops were reunited, when sacrifices wore offered by Alexander for the preservation of his ships and his men, and games were celebrated. Nearkhos, whenever he was seen among the troops, was decorated by them with garlands and pelted with flowers. There also both Nearkhos and Leonnatos were crowned by Alexander with golden diadems—Nearkhos for the safety of the expedition by sea, and Leonnatos for the victory which he had gained over the O r e i t a i and the neighbouring barbarians. It was thus that the expedition which had begun its voyage from the mouths of the Indus was brought in safety to Alexander.

XLIII. Now[112] the parts which lie to the right of the E r y t h r æ a n [113] Sea beyond the realms of Babylonia belong principally to A r a b i a, which extends in one direction as far as the sea that washes the shores of P h œ n i k i a and S y r i a n P a l e s t i n e, while towards sunset it borders on the Egyptians in the direction of the M e d i t e r r a n e a n S e a. Egypt is penetrated by a gulf which extends up from the great ocean, and as this ocean is connected with the E r y t h r æ a n S e a, this fact proves that a voyage could be made all the way from B a b y l o n to E g y p t by means of this gulf. But, owing to the heat and utter sterility of the coast, no one has ever made this voyage, except, it may be, some chance navigator. For the troops belonging to the army of K a m b y s ê s, which escaped from E g y p t, and reached S o u s a in safety, and the troops sent by P t o l e m y, the son of Lagos, to S e l e u k o s N i k a t ô r to B a b y l o n, traversed the Arabian isthmus in eight days altogether.[114] It was a waterless and sterile region, and they had to cross it mounted on swift camels carrying water, travelling only by night, the heat by day being so fierce that they could not expose themselves in the open air. So far are the parts lying beyond this region, which we have spoken of as an isthmus extending from the A r a b i a n G u l f to the E r y t h r æ a n S e a from being inhabited, that even the parts which run up further to the north are a desert of sand. Moreover, men setting forth from the A r a b i a n G u l f in E g y p t, after having sailed round the greater part of A r a b i a to reach the sea which washes the shores of P e r s i s and S o u s a, have returned, after sailing as far along the coast of Arabia as the water they had on board lasted them, and no further. The exploring party again which A l e x a n d e r sent from B a b y l o n with instructions to sail as far as they could along the right-hand coast of the E r y t h r æ a n S e a, with a view to examine the regions lying in that direction, discovered some islands lying in their route, and touched also at certain points of the mainland of A r a b i a. But as for that cape which Nearkhos states to have been seen by the expedition projecting into the sea right opposite to K a r m a n i a, there is no one who has been able to double it and gain the other side. But if the place could possibly be passed, either by sea or by land, it seems to me that Alexander, being so inquisitive and enterprising, would have proved that it could be passed in both these ways.

---

[112] The 3rd part of the *Indika*, the purport of which is to prove that the southern parts of the world are uninhabitable, begins with this chapter.

[113] Here and subsequently meaning the Persian Gulf.

[114] It is not known when or wherefore Ptolemy sent troops on this expedition.

But again H a n n o the L i b y a n , setting out from C a r t h a g e , sailed out into the ocean beyond the Pillars of H e r c u l e s , having L i b y a on his left hand, and the time until his course was shaped towards the rising sun was five-and-thirty days; but when he steered southward he encountered many difficulties from the want of water, from the scorching heat, and from streams of fire that fell into the sea. K y r ê n ê , no doubt, which is situated in a somewhat barren part of L i b y a , is verdant, possessed of a genial climate, and well watered, has groves and meadows, and yields abundantly all kinds of useful animals and vegetable products. But this is only the case up to the limits of the area within which the fennel-plant can grow, while beyond this area the interior of Kyrênê is but a desert of sand.

So ends my narrative relating to A l e x a n d e r , the son of Philip the Makedonian.

INDEX.

C

G

H

I

L

M

Mabber *35*
Macer *11, 28, 29*
Madara *54*
Madeira *10*
Magadoxo *36*
Mahi *60*
Maiôtic Lake *76*
Mais *60*
Maisôlos *75*
Makalleh *48*
Makdashû *36*
Maklow *85, 97*
Makroprosôpoi *74*
Malabar *1, 5, 21, 49, 70, 73*
Malabathrum *11, 12, 13, 75, 76, 77*
Malacca *76*
Malana *80, 85, 98, 99*
Malaô *6, 9, 10, 11, 14, 15, 16, 19, 20, 28, 29, 30*
Malava *91*
Maleus *98*
Malikhos *4*
Malin *98*
Malli *91*
Manaar *73*
Mand *112*
Manda *36*
Mandagora *65, 66*
Mangalur *67*
Manora *82, 84, 95*
Manpalli *72*
Mansura *57*
Mapharitis *3, 41*
Mardians *114*
Margastana *88, 114*
Mariabo *46*
Markah *31*
Markari *69*
Martan *51*
Masalia *74, 75*
Masawwâ *25*
Masira *51*
Maskat *38, 49, 50, 52*
Maṭhurâ *69*
Mazênês *110*

Lector House believes that a society develops through a two-fold approach of continuous learning and adaptation, which is derived from the study of classic literary works spread across the historic timeline of literature records. Therefore, we aim at reviving, repairing and redeveloping all those inaccessible or damaged but historically as well as culturally important literature across subjects so that the future generations may have an opportunity to study and learn from past works to embark upon a journey of creating a better future.

This book is a result of an effort made by Lector House towards making a contribution to the preservation and repair of original ancient works which might hold historical significance to the approach of continuous learning across subjects.

HAPPY READING & LEARNING!

LECTOR HOUSE LLP
E-MAIL: lectorpublishing@gmail.com